A LITTLE BOOK OF SELF CARE

SELF REIKI

TUNE IN TO YOUR LIFE FORCE TO ACHIEVE
HARMONY AND BALANCE

JASMIN HARSONO

Senior Editor Rona Skene
Editor Andrea Page
Senior Designers Mandy Earey,
Collette Sadler
Editorial Assistant Kiron Gill
Senior Producer, Pre-production
Tony Phipps
Senior Producer Luca Bazzoli
Jacket Designer Amy Cox
Jacket Coordinator Lucy Philpott
Creative Technical Support
Sonia Charbonnier
Managing Editor Dawn Henderson
Managing Art Editor Marianne Markham
Art Director Maxine Pedliham
Publishing Director Mary-Clare Jerram

Illustrated by Kotaro Machiyama

First published in Great Britain in 2019 by
Dorling Kindersley Limited
80 Strand, London WC2R 0RL
Copyright © Dorling Kindersley, 2019

A Penguin Random House Company
10 9 8 7 6 5 4 3 2 1
001–316480–December/2019

DISCLAIMER see page 144

A CIP catalogue record for this book is available
from the British Library.

ISBN: 978-0-2414-1038-7

Printed and bound in China

A WORLD OF IDEAS:
SEE ALL THERE IS TO KNOW

www.dk.com

CONTENTS

WELLBEING PRACTICES

HEALING PRACTICES

FOREWORD

Reiki changed my life. The day that I received my first treatment
I felt awakened by a bright light inside me, and after my first
attunement I gradually became aligned to my true self,
passions, and purpose.

My training follows a line back to the founder Mikao Usui, and I am
grateful to have learnt wisdom from inspirational teachers and
mentors across the world. In this book, I want to share some of
that wisdom and also give you a taste of the history and system of
Reiki. But most of all, I want to show you how Reiki can be a
powerful, transformative way to care for and heal yourself. Human
beings are incredible – we are intuitive and our bodies can heal
themselves. Reiki helps us to tap into this innate ability.

In Reiki teaching, healing means to be whole. Our bodies are
made up of four layers – physical, emotional, mental, and spiritual
– and healing needs to take place on all the layers of our being.
When we separate the layers or emphasize one more than the
others we feel unbalanced, constantly yearning for that missing
piece. Through Reiki, we connect to all our layers, we delve
deep into the root of any issue, and we experience love like no
other. In being whole, we shift from loneliness and isolation to
understanding that we are all connected and never alone.

In this book, we have divided the exercises into two themes. In the "Wellbeing" section, you'll find self-Reiki practices and meditations to help you feel and be your best. In "Healing", you will learn techniques and meditations to heal yourself by connecting to the vibrant energy of the universe that's within and around you.

Reiki is for everyone, all living things. I love the feeling that, because of this book, there may be more lights waking up around the world – and our planet, Mother Earth, needs this now more than ever. Reiki is not a religion; it is a healing therapy and spiritual pathway. Through committed daily practice, you will journey deeper and discover what Reiki could mean to you.

If you are new to Reiki, I hope the exercises here will inspire you to find out more and become attuned yourself. If so, you will find details on where to train and receive attunements on pages 138–139. For those already attuned, my Reiki community, I hope this book is something you will carry with you and turn to whenever you need inspiration and support in your self-care.

Sending you light, love, compassion, and kindness as you journey through *Self Reiki*.

With gratitude,
Jasmin Harsono

INTRODUCTION TO REIKI

WHAT IS REIKI?

Reiki (pronounced "ray-key") is a healing art and spiritual practice founded in Japan by Mikao Usui in the early 20th century. By placing hands over the body to share the unseen life-force energy that flows through everyone and everything, we use Reiki to heal, reduce stress, and increase relaxation.

REIKI CHARACTERS

The Japanese Kanji writing system uses two characters for Reiki, expressing the interconnection of heaven and earth energy.

REI

Represents wisdom falling as rain to nourish the earth

The 3 *tandens*

A divine being reaching up for heavenly support

KI

The invisible life-force energy that is everywhere

A grain of rice, which is necessary to sustain human life

WHAT DOES "REIKI" MEAN?

In Japanese, *rei* means "spirit" or "soul" and *ki* means "the energy of the universe". The word can be translated as "universal energy" and also describes the practice of healing with energy. Reiki is more than a complementary therapy for our body, mind, and soul. It can also take us on a journey to inner peace and a more meaningful life. It connects us to all other beings and the universe, and opens a door to our true potential.

" *Reiki connects us to all
other beings and the universe,
and opens a door to
our true potential.* "

HOW DOES REIKI WORK?

Reiki can heal by sharing universal energy to sustain and harmonize the energy field that surrounds us. Anyone can practise Reiki, although you will need to receive training and attunements from a Reiki Master teacher, who will share universal energy with you as part of the Level 1 training. There are three levels of training in the Reiki system, with five elements – this book outlines the basics through practical self-care exercises.

WHAT MAKES REIKI SPECIAL?

Reiki is often described as heaven and earth energy coming together in our hearts, unifying our mind, body, and spirit. The more we practise it, the more we embody oneness, compassion, and kindness. Each soul that connects with Reiki is a star that shares its light throughout the universe. When you heal yourself, you help others too.

REIKI ORIGINS

Today Reiki is practised worldwide, but through its master-to-student teaching tradition we can trace its lineage directly back to its founder, Mikao Usui, and to two key individuals who developed his teachings and spread the practice to the West.

MIKAO USUI

Usui (1865–1926) was born in southern Japan. He was well travelled, with varied intellectual and spiritual interests. After suffering a great loss, he spent time on a mountain near Kyoto in 1922 when he experienced *satori* (a moment of enlightenment). After weeks of fasting and meditation, he felt a profound connection to the entire universe.

While returning home, he injured his foot and instinctively placed his hands over it – to find that the pain disappeared and his foot was completely healed.

Realizing that his awakening had gifted him the ability to heal through his hands, Usui began helping people and developing a teaching system for others to be able to do the same. *Usui Reiki Ryōhō Gakkai* – a society devoted to practising his methods, including the five Reiki elements – was established to enhance spiritual development.

Before his death at the age of 62, Mikao Usui had trained more than 2,000 students and attuned 21 Reiki masters. His memorial stone is at the Saihōji Temple in Tokyo.

" Mikao Usui's awakening had gifted him the ability to heal through his hands. "

DR CHŪJIRŌ HAYASHI

Hayashi (1880–1940) was a Japanese naval medical officer who studied to master level under Usui and later founded his own healing clinic. He further developed the system of Reiki, introducing hand positions for palm healing.

HAWAYO TAKATA

Takata (1900–80) was a Japanese-American born in Hawaii. Whilst in Japan, Takata needed surgery but intuition prompted her to try Reiki first, and over a period of time she was healed.

She decided to stay on in Japan to study under Hayashi, and eventually became the first foreign Master of Reiki. She returned to Hawaii and opened her own clinic, eventually training 22 Reiki masters.

NEW TRADITIONS

Usui integrated Buddhist traditions to develop his system of Reiki, including the Five Principles. Later developments saw variations, such as the use of chakras, integrating with the sytem of Reiki. Takata emphasized healing and introduced daily self-treatments.

REIKI AND ENERGY

To appreciate why Reiki is about connection,
harmony and oneness, you need to understand
the nature of "universal energy".

Science tells us that all matter is made of atoms – each with a nucleus that is filled with energy. So, at the most basic or quantum level, everything is energy and everything is connected.

In Reiki teaching, this energy is called *ki*. It is universal energy, within and around us, vibrating at different frequencies. *Ki* sustains us by supporting the body to vibrate in a constant state of flow, balance and alignment. If we are not aligned, we are disconnected from the physical, mental, emotional, and spiritual aspects of our being, and may experience illness.

Chakras (Sanskrit for "wheels") are energy points that connect our body to our aura – the seven layers of energy that surround and move through our being. The seven main chakras run from the top of the head to the base of the spine, and "spin" to allow *ki* to flow through. Each chakra influences the part of the body where it is located. When our chakras are distributing the optimum amount of energy, we feel balanced and healthy. When they are moving too fast or too slow – for example, due to stress – illness and disease can occur.

Three Diamonds

Universal energy is made up of Earth *ki* and Heaven *ki*. We connect to *ki* through energy centres called *tandens*, often referred to as the Three Diamonds. *Tanden* points are linked to the chakras (see pages 42–43).

UPPER *TANDEN*
is our connection to Heaven *ki*, to our intuition, and to the universe and spirit realm. It corresponds to the Third Eye chakra (see page 46).

MIDDLE *TANDEN*
connects Heaven and Earth *ki* and is home to our passions and purpose. It corresponds to the heart chakra (see page 50).

LOWER *TANDEN (HARA)*
is where we connect to Earth energy and is the home of the body's *ki*, the power centre that supports our basic physical needs and wellbeing. Your *hara* is central to many of the exercises in this book. It corresponds to the sacral chakra (see page 54).

REIKI FOR HEALING

Those who practise Reiki see it as an empowering method of self-care. By connecting to universal energy and following your senses and inner wisdom, you can become your own healer.

Reiki healing begins with the idea that when our life force is disrupted, it can affect us physically, mentally, emotionally, and spiritually. Thoughts, fears, emotions, and experiences can all affect the flow and balance of that force. Self-Reiki clears stagnant, negative energy from the energy field around and inside the body; you may sense Reiki in your palms and hold them over the blocked area, or simply breathe in Reiki to channel its life force and re-balance your flow.

PHYSICAL HEALING
Our physical being is our foundation. When the body is in balance, we feel well, strong, and grounded.

HEALING THE WHOLE
Toxic or slow-moving energy can affect us in different, sometimes unexpected, ways. For example, if we don't feel emotionally supported, this can create tension that manifests as back or shoulder pain. By practising Reiki, we see how the different parts of our being are interconnected.

Healing also means being whole – living with kindness and compassion towards ourselves, others, and the universe. To achieve this level of wellbeing, we pay attention to all four levels of healing.

MENTAL HEALING
This addresses our intellect and decision-making. When the mind is balanced and stimulated, we can think clearly and calmly.

EMOTIONAL HEALING

The emotional realm is one of feelings and reactions, and where we experience life most profoundly. When emotions are balanced, we feel centred and more accepting of ourselves and our past.

SPIRITUAL HEALING

Our spirit is the home of our soul, and where our intuition lies. When this aspect is balanced, it unifies all the others. We feel deeply connected to the universe, and ultimately at one with it.

BENEFITS OF REIKI

Reiki can generate positive change in all aspects of life. Even if you are superficially well, a boost to your energy will help you face life's challenges with more resilience. Reiki healing also supports short-term, chronic and long-term illness and conditions. Reiki practice can help you recognize reactions or thought patterns that hold you back or affect the people around you, so you can strengthen relationships. It can be there when you need to feel calmer or more present in your own life. The self-care exercises in this book may produce immediate healing and transformation, or you may notice effects over time. At first, you may experience a variety of sensations, or you may not feel any difference. Trust that Reiki flows to wherever it is needed, and always towards the higher good.

TRANSFORMATIVE
Can lead to life-changing shifts in mindset; reveals your authentic self and purpose; helps create a more abundant life.

CREATES BALANCE
Tunes into energy on a quantum level; harmonizes physical, mental, emotional, and spiritual layers of your being.

SUPPORTS WELLBEING AND HEALING
Clears blockages and removes unwanted energy so you feel renewed, centred, and more resilient; helps to relieve pain.

SAFE AND COMPLEMENTARY
Reiki is non-intrusive and can be used alongside conventional medicine and other therapies to relieve side effects and promote recovery.

DEEPENS INTUITION
Can be adapted to any situation, challenge, or problem; enriches everyday life and relationships.

DAILY SELF-CARE
Provides deep relaxation and better quality sleep; relieves stress and anxiety; increases mental vitality and clarity.

THE SYSTEM OF REIKI

THE FIVE ELEMENTS

There are five key elements in the system of Reiki – they set out a simple and accessible way to practise self-care and healing. Understanding how the elements fit together will deepen your connection to, and knowledge of, Reiki.

INTRODUCING THE FIVE ELEMENTS

The Five Elements are the fundamental components of the system of Reiki, developed by Mikao Usui. Each element is explained further on the following pages.

ELEMENT 1: REIKI PRINCIPLES
A personal code of practice to help us live positively and mindfully.

ELEMENT 2: MEDITATION
Mindful techniques for creating a more profound connection to Reiki.

ELEMENT 3: HEALING HANDS
Using the palms to share *ki* and offer healing to ourselves and others.

ELEMENT 4: ATTUNEMENTS
Rituals to share universal energy with the recipient, and help them develop their knowledge and connection.

ELEMENT 5: SYMBOLS AND MANTRAS
These are used with the attunements to share and build knowledge of Reiki.

A PRACTICAL SYSTEM
Mikao Usui developed the system of Five Elements to be used on a daily basis. Newcomers to Reiki will mainly be concerned with the first three elements: on pages 42–57 you will begin implementing these in performing a full Reiki treatment on yourself. The elements also underpin all the wellbeing and self-healing exercises in the rest of the book, supporting your body and mind, and helping you to develop your spiritual self.

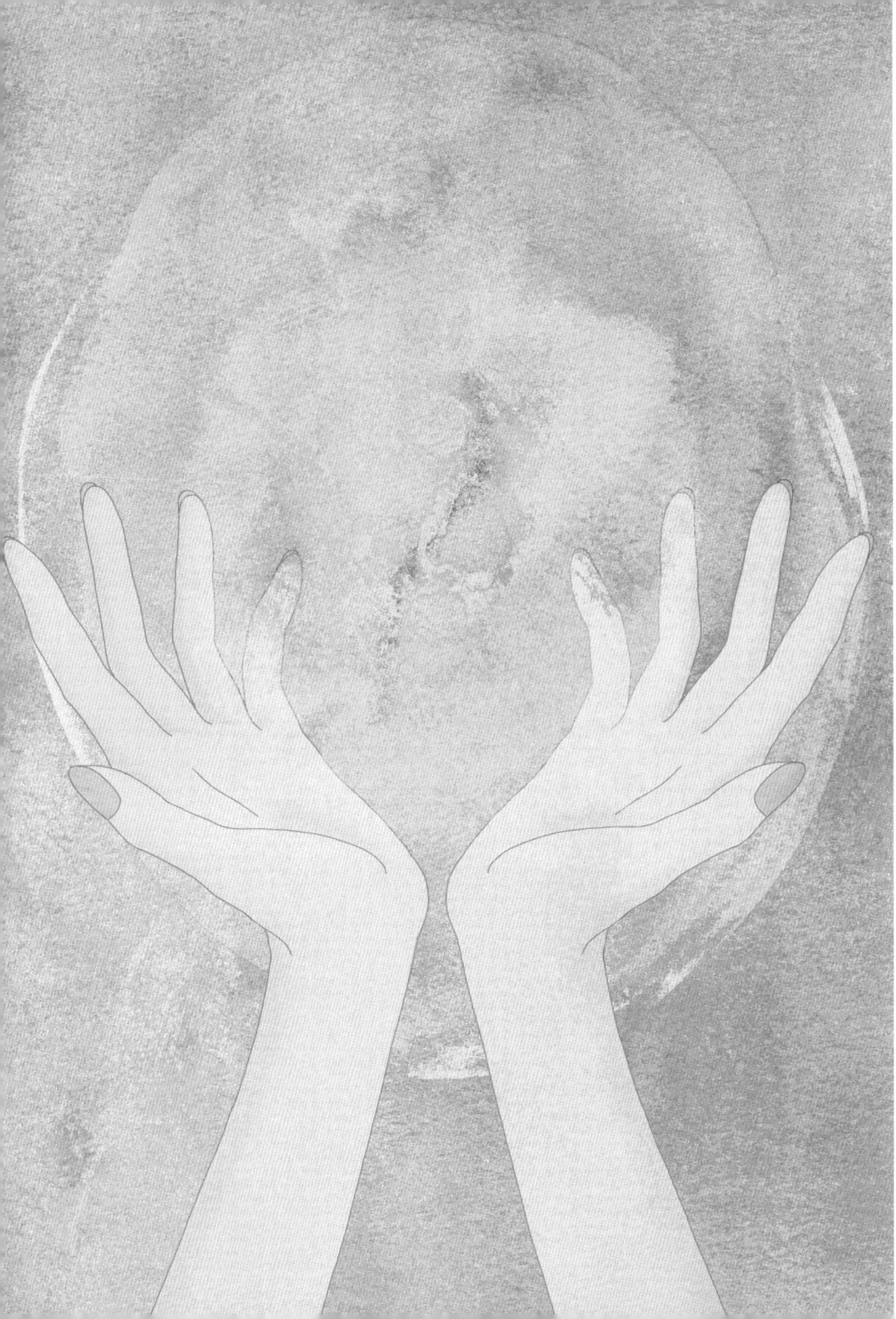

REIKI PRINCIPLES

The Reiki principles (*Gokai*) were created to help us to shift our perspective, live in the moment, and love and respect ourselves and others. Aim to recite them every morning and evening for five minutes each. This requires patience, but it will help you live mindfully and create more positive outcomes. For example, by saying "do not anger" you can let anger surface, consciously observe it, then let the feeling pass. In this way you can understand it is only the ego that wants us to hold onto things that do not serve our true self. As you practise, keep a journal of any emotions, messages, and changes that arise.

... do not anger

This principle helps you discover what lies beneath your anger, and find other, more helpful ways to express negative emotions.

... do not worry

Life will always present obstacles, but worrying can ultimately take us further away from love. This principle is challenging, but helps you to trust in outcomes.

... be grateful

Counting even our
smallest blessings every day
"rewires" the mind positively.

... work
with diligence

This principle helps you to
navigate life with ease and flow;
giving any activity your complete
attention demonstrates respect
for it, and yourself.

Just for today...

Saying this at the beginning
of each principle reminds us to
be in the present moment.

... be kind to
yourself and others

Love is the essence of Reiki. Being
kind without judgement strengthens
our ability to live with passion and
purpose, knowing that we are
all connected.

MEDITATION

Reiki is a beautiful, meditative practice. We meditate to open ourselves to *ki* and deepen our connection to Reiki, which in turn guides us towards inner peace and ultimately, the true self.

Meditation is simply the bringing of your awareness and practice completely into the here and now.

The more you can achieve a mentally clear, emotionally calm, harmonious state of being, the more profound your connection with Reiki will be. This means accepting any worries or doubts you have about achieving this state. Meditation can take practice and patience, especially at first. If you feel restless or if random, distracting thoughts enter your mind, know that this is OK. Practise anchoring yourself in the present by bringing attention to your breathing. There may be some resistance; try to accept the experience as it is, and continue with your practice until the end of your meditation.

You can meditate at any time or place. Two elements of meditation that can aid

SETTING INTENTIONS

Intention is essential to Reiki meditation. When you begin, consciously set an intention to be fully present in the experience. You can add in what you want to happen – by doing this, you show your trust that universal energy will flow where it needs to.

FEELING A CONNECTION

Meditations such as *gasshō* (see pages 30–31) help us to connect to Reiki. Sensing Reiki could feel like a warmth in your palms, a heightened feeling of energy around you, or another sensation altogether – it's personal to you and different for everyone.

" *Practise anchoring yourself in the present by bringing attention to your breathing.* "

your practice and help you focus are posture and breathing. The starting point for many of the exercises and meditations in this book is connecting to *gasshō* (see pages 30–31). Adopting this hands-together pose is a powerful practice that helps you also connect to Reiki. Other meditations that are recommended for use with other exercises include *Kenyoku Hō* ("dry bathing") (see pages 60–61)

and *Hatsurei Hō* ("purifying the spirit") (see pages 62–63). Dry bathing cleanses your energy channels, both before and after another meditation, while the purifying meditation uses the breath to release negativity, extending and deepening your spiritual practice.

MEDITATION

Posture

Gasshō ("hands coming together") is the starting point for many exercises in this book. It describes the posture that you adopt to connect to Reiki, centring your energy and bringing *yin* and *yan* together. Holding the hands together helps you to focus and unites Heaven *ki* and Earth *ki* within your heart.

SITTING COMFORTABLY

Wherever you choose to meditate, it is crucially important that you are comfortable. You can kneel, sit cross-legged, or sit on a chair with your feet flat on the floor. Always make sure your spine is tall and straight, so Reiki can flow easily. *Seiza* is a traditional Japanese meditation posture; kneeling flat on the lower legs and knees, with your bottom on the floor between the feet, soles pointing upwards.

01

Sit quietly and comfortably with your spine straight; either cross-legged, in a chair, or in *seiza*. Close your eyes and breathe slowly through your nose.

02

Put your hands together with palms and fingers touching, and place them on or over the middle of your chest, covering your heart.

03

Stay like this for at least 5 minutes, until you sense Reiki flowing into your hands. Focus on your breathing, or on your middle fingertips touching.

04

To finish, thank Reiki, open your eyes and relax your hands.

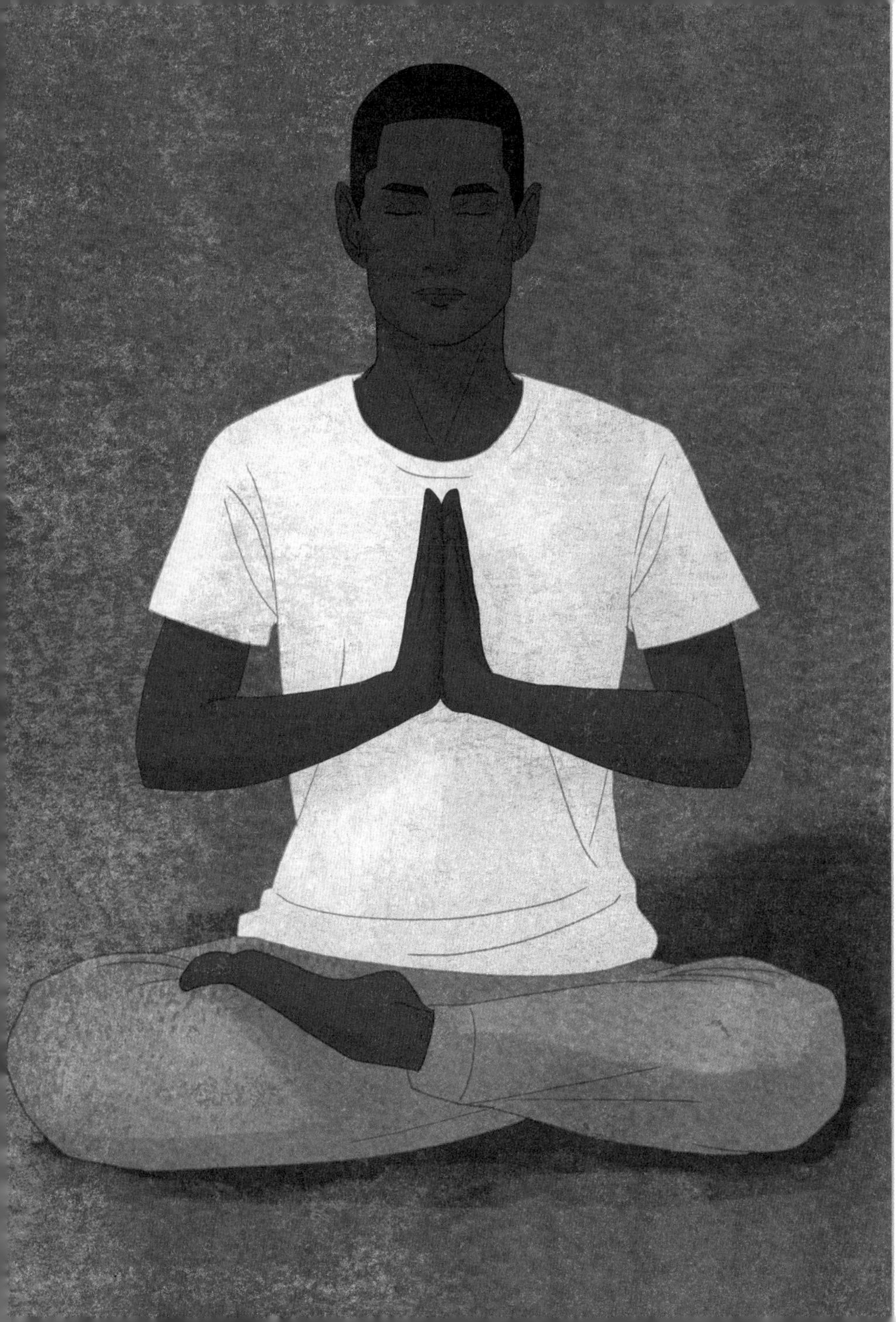

MEDITATION
Breathing

Breath is central to Reiki meditation. Practise controlling and expanding your breath to enhance your connection between mind, body, and spirit.

As we meditate, we breathe Reiki in with the air, and visualize it flowing into us and infusing our being. With our out-breaths, we release anything that no longer serves us. Practise sensing Reiki filling you with each breath.

Unless directed otherwise, you can choose how to breathe: breathing through the nose relaxes and balances, while mouth breathing releases and energizes. Or you can breathe in through the nose and out through the mouth – and vice versa. Start your meditation by becoming aware of your breathing, the sensations you have as you breathe, and the rise and fall of your body.

BREATHE INTO YOUR *HARA*
Some exercises in this book ask you to breathe into your *hara* – your body's physical core and main energy source, located in your lower abdomen (see pages 54–55).

We guide the breath here to feel centred in mind, body, and spirit and to achieve a strong connection to *ki*. First, inhale deeply through your nose down into your core, inflating the belly. Extend the in-breath, keeping the belly inflated, to fill the lungs and the rest of your body with air and Reiki. Then exhale, using your stomach muscles to slowly and fully push out the breath.

USE YOUR HANDS
Sometimes you are asked to breathe through your hands or into a particular chakra or energy centre. In this case, you continue to breathe through the nose or mouth, but by placing your hands as directed, you amplify your connection through the mixture of your breathing, your intention, and the *ki* that also flows from your palms (see pages 34–35).

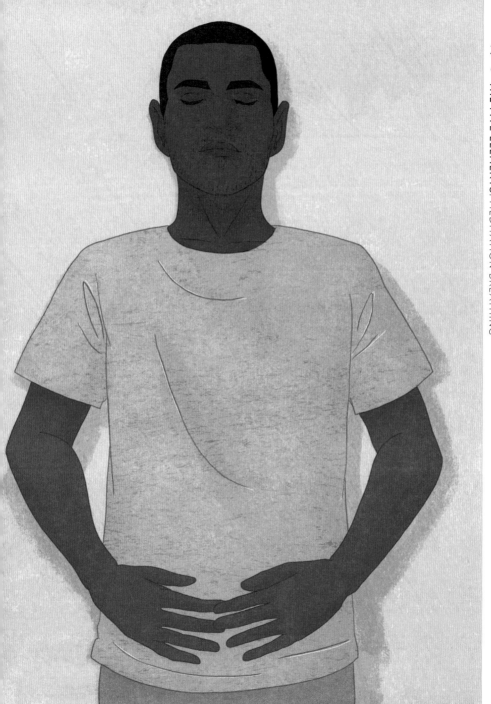

HEALING HANDS

The third element in the system of Reiki is palm healing, or *tenohira*. This is the technique of sharing *ki* through the palms to heal ourselves and others, or simply to feel its beneficial energy.

The power of touch is as ancient as humanity; when we hurt ourselves, we instinctively cover or rub the injured area, and when someone else is in pain, we reach out to them to offer comfort. The hands are where many people first feel their connection with life-force energy. When you connect to Reiki, your hands may tingle, become warmer, or feel heavier or lighter. We can also use the hands to share *ki*.

PLACING HANDS

Practising the hand positions for the complete Reiki self-treatment (see pages 42–57) will help you get used to sharing Reiki with your palms. Remember, your hands are simply a conduit for Reiki energy, as it flows through you to where it is needed.

FOLLOW YOUR INTUITION

As you get more accustomed to performing Reiki palm healing on yourself, you may start to feel a pull to stay a little longer in one position, or to move on to treat another area that you hadn't realized needed attention. This is your intuition working. Trust your inner voice, and be guided by Reiki.

01

Put your hands in *gasshō* (see pages 30–31), breathe deeply into your *hara* (see pages 32–33), and close your eyes. Connect with Reiki and wait to sense it in your hands. If you don't feel anything, trust that it is present.

02

Place your palms over or lightly touching the area that may need healing; spend at least 5 minutes in this position, noticing any changes in how you feel. To finish, thank Reiki.

ATTUNEMENTS

Before you can use Reiki for self-care, you must
be awakened to the presence of universal energy.
This happens through an element of the system
called attunement.

Attunement is a ritual in which a Reiki master shares universal energy with their student. It is used in the western lineage (*usui shiki ryōhō*) of Reiki teaching, the most widely used system worldwide. Attunements are woven throughout the system of Reiki teaching, and are used together with symbols and mantras (see pages 38–39).

The eastern lineage (*usui reiki ryōhō*) often offers a simple blessing from master to student, called *reiju*. *Reijus* are also used as a blessing to share *ki* when a Reiki community gathers together.

Attunement and *reijus* are designed to bring us back to the universal energy that is constantly within and around us. From the moment you are first attuned to Reiki, you will always be able to access and connect to it.

If you choose to develop your Reiki practice, each of the teaching levels will explore different aspects of the Five Elements, and offer different attunements.

"*Attunements awaken us to the universal energy that is constantly within and around us.*"

REIKI LEVELS AND ATTUNEMENTS

Level 1 (*Shoden*) Students learn to sense, connect to, and cultivate Reiki; grounding and self-healing; attunements allow you to share Reiki with yourself and others on a personal basis.

Level 2 (*Okuden*) This level builds knowledge of the Five Elements; strengthens connection to Reiki; reveals symbols and mantras that bring greater focus; attunements enable the recipient to give distant healing; enhances meditation with additional techniques.

Level 3 (*Shinpiden*) Master/teacher level that deepens personal development, understanding of the Five Elements and of the universe; attunements enable the recipient to teach and attune others to Reiki.

SYMBOLS AND MANTRAS

Symbols *(shirushi)*, together with their related mantras *(jumon)*, work together as the fourth element of the Reiki system. They are used by Reiki students and practitioners who have achieved Level 2 and beyond in Reiki teaching.

The four symbols were created to help students to focus on and intensify their connection with Reiki, and to invoke specific kinds of healing energy. They are also used as part of a sound-healing meditation practice.

Each symbol is usually activated by drawing it in the air and saying the mantra – and repeating three times. The mantra is the phrase in the Japanese Kanji writing form that expresses the symbol's essence. The *kotodama* ("language of spirit") involves chanting the phonetic vowel sounds of each mantra, silently or aloud; this holds immense healing power, and connects to a precise cosmic vibration.

POWER SYMBOL

MANTRA *Cho Ku Rei* (pronounced "choo koo ray")

KOTODAMA "O-U-E-I"

CONNECTION Earth *ki*, nature

WHEN IT IS USED Evokes masculine and feminine energy; connects us to innate power; cuts through problems; healing physical issues.

HARMONY SYMBOL

MANTRA *Sei He Ki*
(pronounced "say heh kee")

KOTODAMA "E-I-E-KI"

CONNECTION Heaven *ki*

WHEN IT IS USED Evokes energy to heal emotional and mental issues; develops intuition and psychic connection; brings harmony.

CONNECTION SYMBOL

MANTRA *Hon Sha Ze Sho Nen*
(pronounced "Hon shar ze show nen")

KOTODAMA "(H)O-A-ZE-(H)O-NE"

CONNECTION
Heart *ki*,
oneness

WHEN IT IS USED
Helps connect
us to our true self
and all living
things; allows us
to send Reiki
remotely after
attunement.

GREAT BRIGHT LIGHT SYMBOL

MANTRA *Dai Kōmyō*
(pronounced "die ko-me-oh")

KOTODAMA "A-I-KO-YO"

CONNECTION True, authentic self

WHEN IT IS USED
Connects us to the
source of Reiki, and
a state of *satori*
(enlightenment).

FULL TREATMENT

In conjunction with the Five Elements,
the full treatment is a foundation for
your self-healing practice. Using your
hands to access your body's main
chakras, you allow life-force energy
to flow to every layer of your being.

FULL TREATMENT

Performing a full Reiki self-treatment every day will help you to tune inwards and notice any energy blockages affecting your body, mind, or spirit. You can then follow up with other treatments and meditations to address specific concerns.

A full treatment is an excellent way to begin your Reiki practice. This treatment is based on the seven main chakras – the following pages show you where to place your hands.

After a full treatment you may feel calm, refreshed, and alert, and be able to sleep better. Or, as your emotions are heightened, you may feel tired. Trust that Reiki is supporting you, continue your practice, and allow time for the body to adjust.

NEED TO KNOW

BENEFITS Releases blockages, pain, and tension; creates balance and harmony; deepens meditation; prepares for other treatments.

TIME 40 minutes, at any time that's convenient.

PREPARATION Find a comfortable space. Start by performing dry bathing (see pages 60–61).

01

Lie on your back with your feet spread apart. Close your eyes and place your hands in *gasshō* (see pages 30–31). Take deep, slow breaths in through your nose and out through your mouth. Continue until you can sense Reiki.

02

Place your hands on or above your crown chakra (see pages 44–45) and share Reiki for a minimum of 3–5 minutes.

03

Work down the body, repeating step 2 for each of the other chakras, in the order shown on pages 44–57.

04

Finish by placing your hands in *gasshō* and thanking Reiki. End with more dry bathing.

Know your chakras

There are seven main chakra energy points. Each one is linked to healing a different aspect of our physical, mental, emotional, and spiritual being.

CROWN CHAKRA
pages 44–45

THIRD EYE
CHAKRA
pages 46–47

THROAT CHAKRA
pages 48–49

HEART CHAKRA
pages 50–51

SOLAR
PLEXUS CHAKRA
pages 52–53

SACRAL CHAKRA
pages 54–55

ROOT CHAKRA
pages 56–57

Continued ▶▶

FULL TREATMENT 1
Crown chakra

This chakra is our connection to heaven energy and through it, to our own higher consciousness. Invite Reiki to elevate your spiritual awareness and experience a sense of oneness with the universe. In time, this will help you to let go of ego and discover your authentic self.

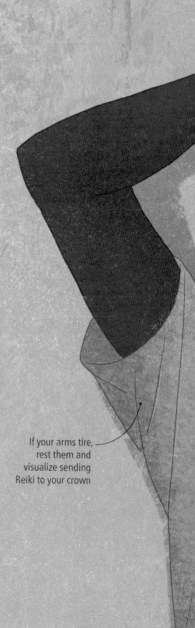

If your arms tire, rest them and visualize sending Reiki to your crown

CHAKRA LOCATOR

The crown chakra is located at the very top of the head. This chakra is linked to the brain, the nervous system, and to overall health.

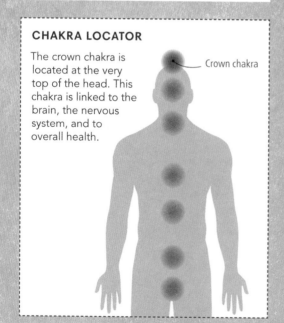

Crown chakra

Hands side-by-side
on or above the top
of your head

Continued ▶▶

FULL TREATMENT 2
Third Eye chakra

This is the chakra of higher wisdom and intuition. By connecting and sharing Reiki through this energy point, you will be able to strengthen your intuition and call on this inner voice when you need to, and receive guidance from the spirit realm.

CHAKRA LOCATOR

The Third Eye is situated on your forehead, between your eyebrows, and is known as the Upper *Tanden* in Reiki (see pages 14–15). It is linked to vision, hearing, and the pineal gland, which regulates hormones.

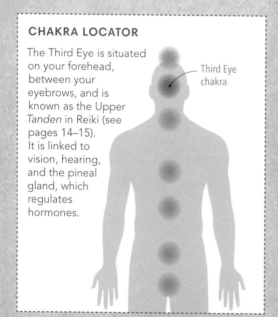

Third Eye chakra

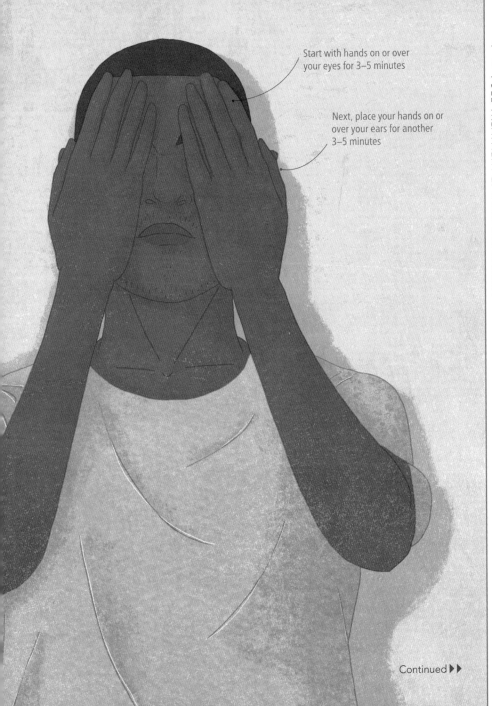

Start with hands on or over your eyes for 3–5 minutes

Next, place your hands on or over your ears for another 3–5 minutes

Continued ▶▶

FULL TREATMENT 3
Throat chakra

This is the chakra of self-expression and communication, both physical and emotional. Sharing Reiki by placing hands on or over your throat chakra helps to relieve muscle tension and clear energy blockages there, allowing you to express yourself more openly and effectively.

CHAKRA LOCATOR

The throat chakra sits on the neck, beneath your chin. It is the emotional hub and links to the thyroid gland and endocrine system.

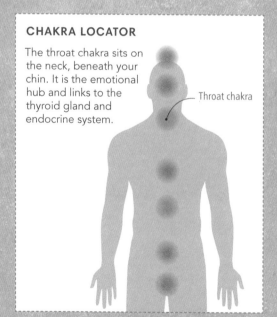

Throat chakra

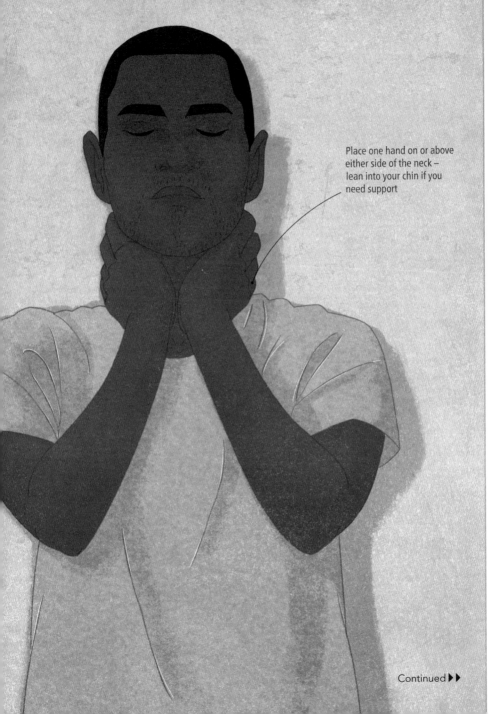

Place one hand on or above either side of the neck – lean into your chin if you need support

Continued ▶▶

FULL TREATMENT 4

Heart chakra

This is the chakra of unconditional love and the point where Heaven and Earth *ki* meet in your being. Sharing Reiki to the Heart *ki* restores balance, cultivates compassion, and helps you to relieve negative emotions such as jealousy and anger. It also lets you tap into your creativity and discover your true purpose.

CHAKRA LOCATOR

Your heart chakra is located in the centre of your chest, and is linked to heart health, lungs, and breathing. It shares its location with the Middle *Tanden* in Reiki (see pages 14–15).

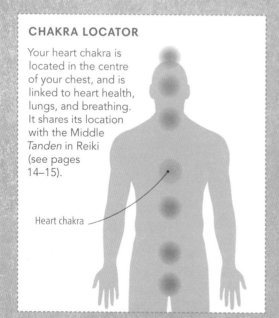

Heart chakra

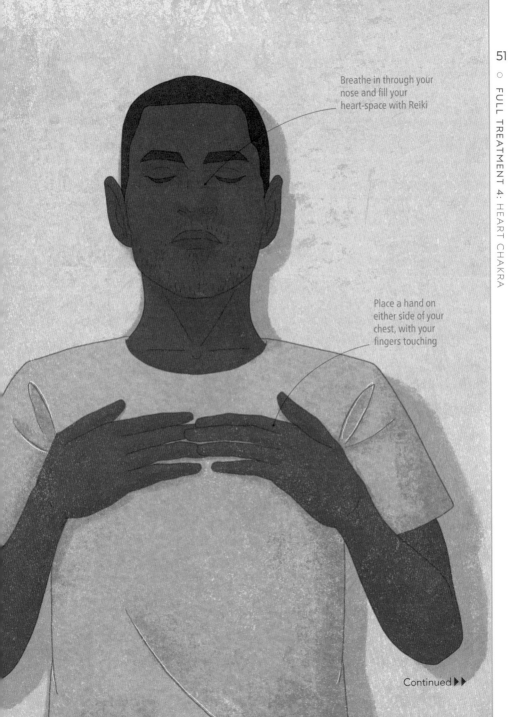

Breathe in through your nose and fill your heart-space with Reiki

Place a hand on either side of your chest, with your fingers touching

Continued ▶▶

FULL TREATMENT 5

Solar plexus chakra

This is the chakra of self-esteem, empowerment, and focus. Sharing Reiki energy to this chakra helps to address issues relating to depression, indecision, and willpower, so that you can regain self-confidence and step into your personal power.

Throughout the treatment, use out-breaths to let go of any feelings and emotions that no longer serve you

CHAKRA LOCATOR

The solar plexus chakra is located in the middle of your torso, a few inches above your navel and below your breastbone. It is also linked to digestive health.

Solar plexus chakra

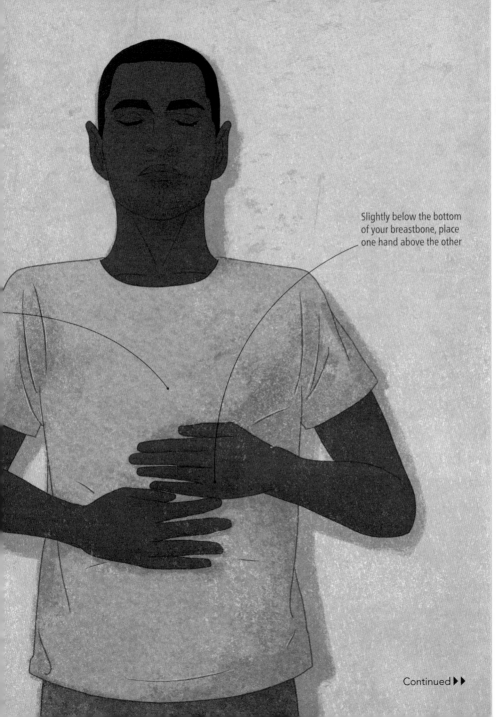

Slightly below the bottom of your breastbone, place one hand above the other

Continued ▶▶

FULL TREATMENT 6
Sacral chakra (*hara*)

This chakra is the seat of the body's primary energy centre in Reiki – the *hara* – which is the home of our Earth *ki*. It powers emotional intelligence, sexuality, creativity, balance, and pleasure. It is key to feeling empowered and connected to love without fear or judgement.

CHAKRA LOCATOR

Your sacral chakra/*hara* sits just below your belly button. It links to reproductive organs and intestinal health. It shares its location with the Lower *Tanden* in Reiki (see pages 14–15).

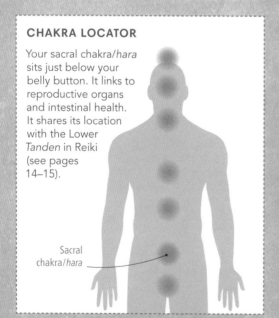

Sacral chakra/*hara*

If your stomach gurgles, it's usually a sign that Reiki energy is flowing

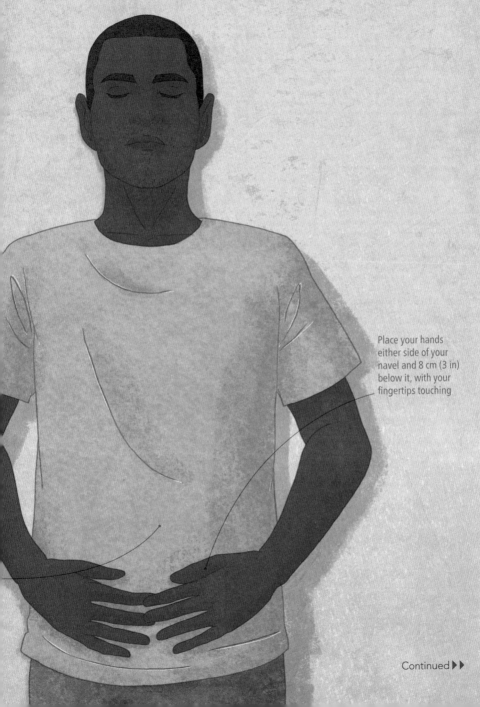

Place your hands either side of your navel and 8 cm (3 in) below it, with your fingertips touching

Continued ▶▶

FULL TREATMENT 7

Root chakra

The root chakra supports the weight of the body's real-world needs and is the seat of our sense of security. Sharing Reiki here allows us to feel more confident and self-reliant, which is the essential bedrock for our wellbeing.

CHAKRA LOCATOR

The root chakra sits at the base of the spine, grounding us. It is linked with the health of the reproductive organs, legs, back, feet, and the immune system.

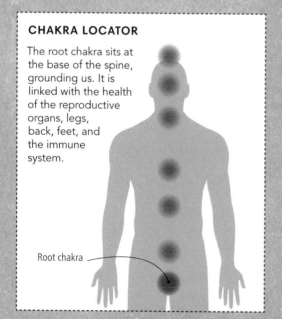

Root chakra

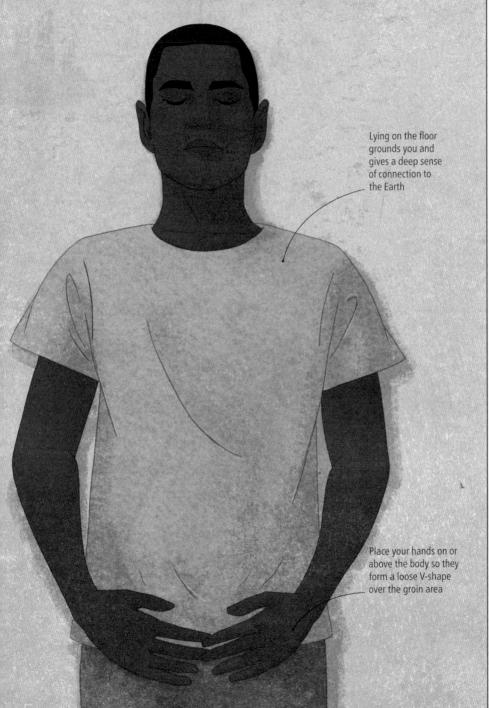

Lying on the floor grounds you and gives a deep sense of connection to the Earth

Place your hands on or above the body so they form a loose V-shape over the groin area

WELLBEING PRACTICES

DRY BATHING FOR ENERGY CLEANSING

Known as *Kenyoku Hō* ("dry bathing"), this exercise consists of six very swift brushing movements, each accompanied by a short in-breath through the nose. Use it when you feel tired or depleted, before a stressful event such as an interview, and before and after you connect with or share Reiki.

NEED TO KNOW

BENEFITS Symbolically cleanses the body's channels, allowing *ki* to flow more easily.

TIME About 30 seconds – this exercise should be performed briskly.

BEFORE YOU BEGIN To prepare, centre yourself by taking three deep, slow breaths, all the way into your *hara*.

01

Place your right hand on your left shoulder. Inhale through the nose and make a swift diagonal stroke across your body to your right hip. Without exhaling, take another in-breath and sweep your left hand from right shoulder to left hip. Inhale again and repeat the first action.

02

Hold your left arm out. Still without exhaling, quickly draw your right hand down your arm. Inhale again and sweep your right arm with your left hand.

03

Taking one last nose breath, sweep your left arm again with your right hand. Exhale fully to finish.

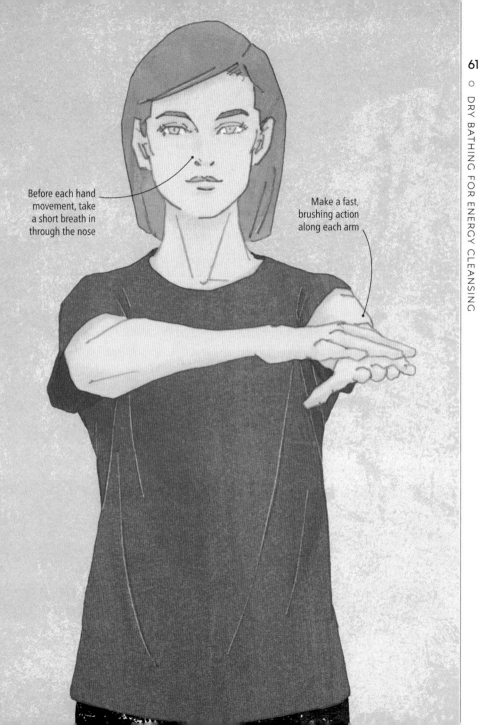

Before each hand movement, take a short breath in through the nose

Make a fast, brushing action along each arm

PURIFICATION MEDITATION

This exercise is adapted from a technique called *Hatsurei Hō* ("purifying the spirit"). As you carry out this breathing exercise, toxins are released from all levels of your being. As stagnant energy is released, memories or emotions can resurface, or you may experience a variety of physical symptoms. Allow time for these to pass; trust in the process and be guided by your breath.

01

Close your eyes and place your hands on your thighs with your palms facing down.

NEED TO KNOW

BENEFITS Helps you to feel centred and whole, and to let go of anything that no longer serves you.

TIME 15–20 minutes.

PREPARATION Sit with your feet planted firmly on the ground and perform the dry-bathing exercise (see pages 60–61). Connect to *gasshō* (see pages 30–31).

02

Take deep slow breaths into your *hara* and sense Reiki flowing and expanding. With each exhale, let go of what needs to be released, and visualize the energy growing within you.

03

Keep breathing in Reiki this way until you experience purifying light filling all the layers of your being. Extend this light into your space, and then the whole planet.

04

Draw to a close by placing your hands in *gasshō*. Take three deep breaths in through your hands into your heart-space. Finish by thanking Reiki and repeating the dry-bathing exercise.

Place your
hands on your
knees, palms up

RESTORE YOUR BALANCE

This ritual helps to shut out distractions that may be preventing you from feeling centred. Perform it whenever you feel disconnected or out of balance.

NEED TO KNOW

BENEFITS Develops inner peace; a sense of balance in every layer of your being.

TIME 15–20 minutes, or longer if needed.

ITEMS NEEDED 8 tea lights.

PREPARATION In a quiet, darkened space, place the tea lights in a circle on the floor and light them.

FURTHER PRACTICE After step 2, Reiki 2+ practitioners may choose to draw the power symbol (see pages 38–39), transfer the symbol into the circle, and repeat the mantra three times.

01

Stand outside the circle and perform dry bathing (see pages 60–61). Close your eyes, put your hands in *gasshō* and connect to Reiki. Visualize Reiki energy filling your being, extending and connecting to the flames, and filling the circle with bright, healing light.

02

Open your eyes and carefully step into the circle. Sit with palms open and feel the energy of Reiki. Stay present with your breath as you bathe in the sphere of light and fire encircling you.

03

Stay in this space until you feel completely balanced. Then carefully step out of the circle and finish with more dry bathing. Put your hands in *gasshō*, thank Reiki, and blow out the candles.

02

As you exhale through your nose, send Reiki through every cell of your being, then out of your body and into the space around you. Feel your physical body sinking deeper into the earth.

01

Close your eyes and place your hands on your *hara*. Breathe in deeply through your nose into your *hara*. As Reiki flows in with the air, it expands and fills your entire being. Feel your body rising upward.

CREATE INNER HARMONY

Our breath is naturally healing, yet we rarely take time to breathe fully into our being. This meditation guides us to understand that the universe is part of us, by deeply breathing its life-force energy. It is called *Jōshin Kokyū Hō*, which means "connection to the pure mind and heart through harmony with the universe".

03

After a few breaths, place your hands on your lap with your palms facing upwards. Continue the steady flow of breath in and out of your nose.

04

If you feel resistance to settling into the exercise, be patient; with each breath you will feel more grounded. After 10 minutes or when you feel ready, finish by placing your hands in *gasshō* and thanking Reiki.

NEED TO KNOW

BENEFITS Clears blocked energy pathways; a sense of oneness, that there is no separation between us and the universe.

TIME 10 minutes, building up to 30 minutes or more.

PREPARATION Sit upright, with your feet flat on the ground. Put your hands in *gasshō* (see pages 30–31) and connect to Reiki, breathing in through your nose and out through your mouth.

CAUTION If you start to feel dizzy at any time, return to normal breathing. Begin again only when you feel fully recovered.

ACHIEVE FOCUS AND CLARITY

This technique, called "Reiki Shower", increases energy flow into the mind, body, and spirit. This is a short but powerful exercise, in which you sense the energy as it flows over and through you like cleansing, refreshing water.

NEED TO KNOW

BENEFITS Bringing attention to the flow of energy encourages clarity; relieves tiredness and improves concentration.

TIME 2–3 minutes.

PREPARATION Sit or stand in a quiet, private space. Connect to *gasshō* (see pages 30–31) and breathe in and out into your *hara*.

01

Close your eyes and reach your hands high up above your head. Make a cup shape with your hands. Feel the connection of Reiki as it flows through your hands and into your headspace.

02

As the energy reaches your shoulders, bring your hands down in front of your body. With the downward movement of your hands, sense the energy flowing down your body.

03

Visualize Reiki as water, cleansing every part of you. As it reaches the ground, visualize stagnant energy being taken in by the earth and recycled into renewed life energy.

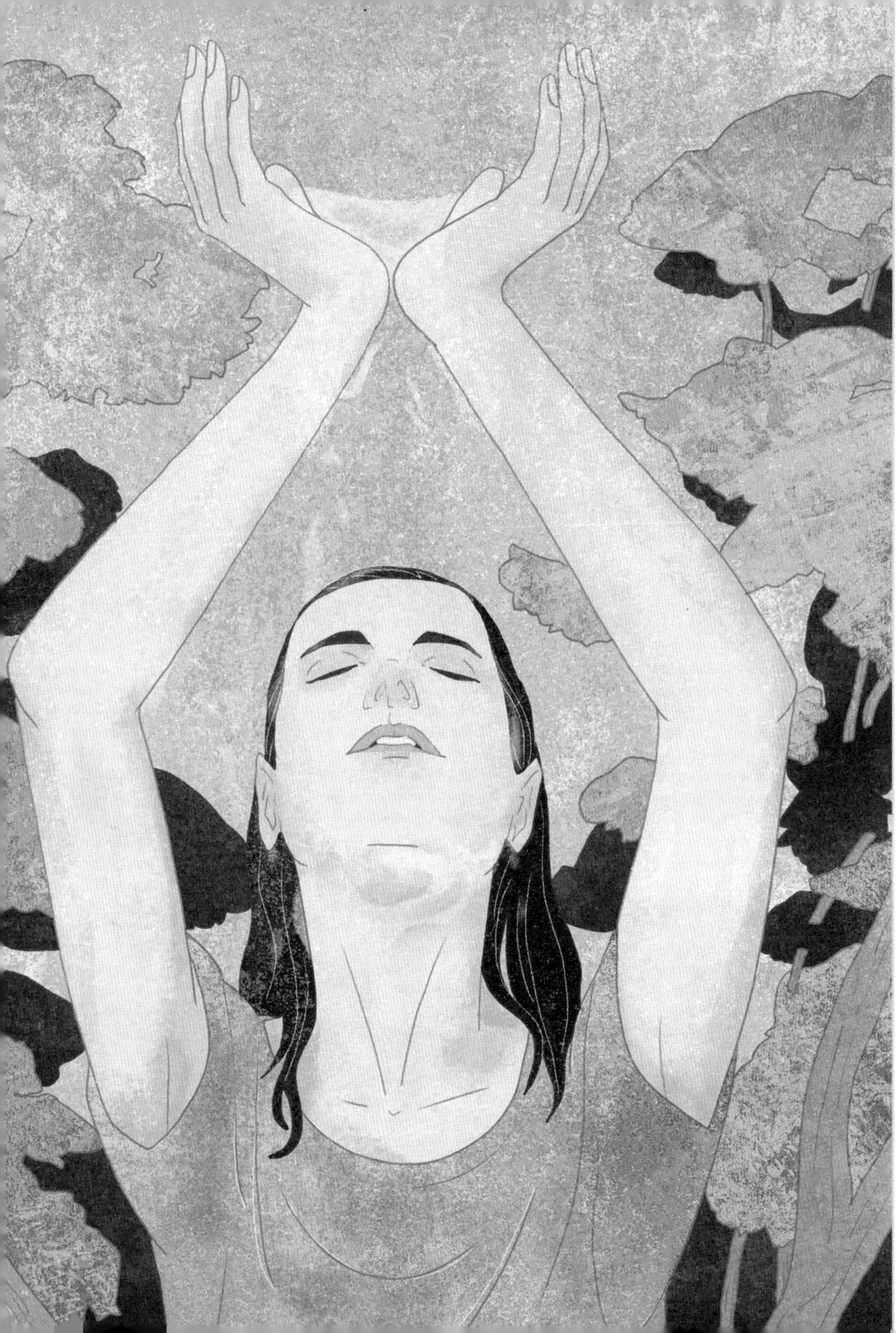

02

Now, visualize sending Reiki energy directly to the situation or challenge. Continue for at least 3–5 minutes, feeling the connection between you.

01

Sit or stand and take a deep breath into your *hara*. Close your eyes and as you inhale, set an intention for how you want this situation to turn out, trusting in Reiki to support the best outcome.

OVERCOME CHALLENGES

When we are faced with problems, challenges, or difficult decisions, we can connect to universal energy for support. Use this meditation to set a positive goal and activate Reiki to flow towards it, trusting that Reiki will go to the highest good.

03

Believe that Reiki is always
present and supporting you;
the more you feel this, the
more connection you will have
to your intended pathway.

04

When you feel ready, open
your eyes. Repeat the
dry-bathing exercise, bring
your hands together in
gasshō, and thank Reiki.

NEED TO KNOW

BENEFITS Self-belief; trust that, in sending with the best
intention, things will turn out as they should.

TIME 7–10 minutes.

PREPARATION Perform dry bathing (see pages 60–61). Place
your hands in *gasshō* (see pages 30–31) and connect with Reiki.

FURTHER PRACTICE Reiki 2+ practitioners can apply the power
symbol before step 2 (see pages 38–39).

02

Place the intentions, along with the principles, crystals, and totems (if using) in the box. Close the lid and place the box in front of you.

01

Think of the things you would like to call into your life. Write them in a list – you can also use images and objects to represent your intentions. Now make a list of the 5 Reiki principles (see pages 26–27).

MANIFESTATION RITUAL

This practice has you gathering intentions together, so that you can share Reiki energy with them whenever you need to. You can manifest an abundant life, in whatever way is meaningful to you, by connecting with universal energy and taking action for the life you want to create.

04

Take time to connect to the feeling that you are manifesting an abundant life right here and now. Place your hands on or over the box, infusing it and its contents with Reiki. Recite the Reiki principles three times.

03

Close your eyes, connect to *gasshō* and sense Reiki (see pages 30–31). Take deep, slow breaths into your *hara*. Use all your senses and belief to visualize the list of intentions being sent into the universe to begin its creation into form.

05

Finish by placing your hands in *gasshō*, and giving thanks to Reiki for all that you have in your life at this present time.

NEED TO KNOW

BENEFITS Feel empowered; reduce stress and procrastination.

TIME 90 minutes.

ITEMS NEEDED Box with lid, large enough to hold crystals and totems; crystals: citrine for abundance, aventurine for purpose, clear quartz for amplifying intention; paper and pen.

PREPARATION Clear your space of negative energy (see pages 102–103).

FURTHER PRACTICE Reiki 2+ practitioners may use the power symbol after step 4 (see pages 38–39).

GRATITUDE JOURNALLING

Writing is a powerful healing tool, and keeping a gratitude journal helps us to be mindful of all that is good in our lives. Performing this exercise every day reminds you of the Reiki principle of staying present with gratitude.

NEED TO KNOW

BENEFITS Encourages a state of high vibrational energy; cultivates kindness and a deep sense of awareness.

TIME 10–15 minutes; longer if needed.

ITEMS NEEDED Journal or exercise book; pen.

PREPARATION Write your name inside the journal, then the Reiki principle, "Just for today, I am grateful". In a quiet space, put your hands in *gasshō* and connect with Reiki (see pages 30–31).

FURTHER PRACTICE Reiki 2+ practitioners can draw the connection symbol after step 1 (see pages 38–39).

01

Breathe deeply into your *hara*. Read out the Reiki principle three times. Visualize a sphere of white light around and within you.

02

Continue to breathe deeply. Write the date, then list all the things you feel grateful for. Write intuitively; don't analyse what comes to you.

03

When you are ready to finish, close the book. Place your hand on it and share Reiki, visualizing what you are grateful for in the present moment.

04

Place your hands in *gasshō* and thank Reiki by reciting the gratitude principle again.

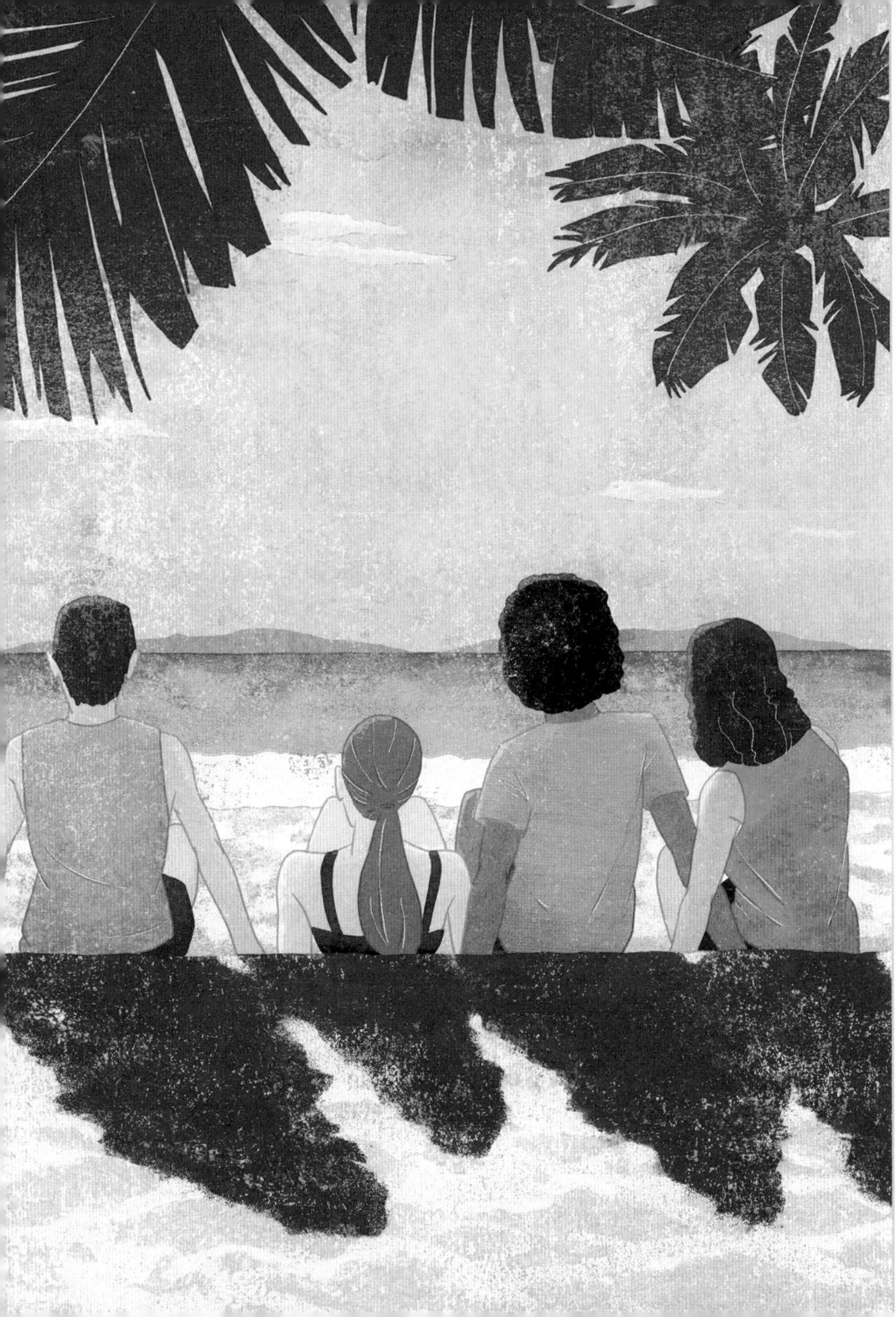

WATER RITUAL BLESSING

Water is life: it nourishes our cells, organs, and tissues, is at the heart of all the the body's most essential functions, and keeps us cool, clean, healthy, and alert. This exercise infuses your water with vital life-force energy – use it for drinking, to cleanse your skin, feed your plants, share with friends, or create a room spray to clear negativity in your space.

NEED TO KNOW

BENEFITS The ritual helps us to be mindful of how precious water is to us and our planet; Reiki water detoxifies and purifies the body and spirit.

TIME Up to 1 hour. Blessing lasts for up to a week.

ITEMS NEEDED As many glass bottles as needed, filled with water.

PREPARATION Prepare your space by clearing it of negative energy (see pages 102–103). Set out your bottles of water.

01

Sit or stand comfortably. Start by performing the dry-bathing exercise (see pages 60–61). Connect to *gasshō* (see pages 30–31) and sense Reiki.

02

Place your hands on or above the bottles. Intend to send the healing vibrations of Reiki to the water, removing any impurities or pollution and imparting each atom with Reiki life energy. Spend 15–60 minutes blessing the water.

03

Pour a little water to drink and end in *gasshō*. Thank Reiki by saying: "Just for today, I am grateful".

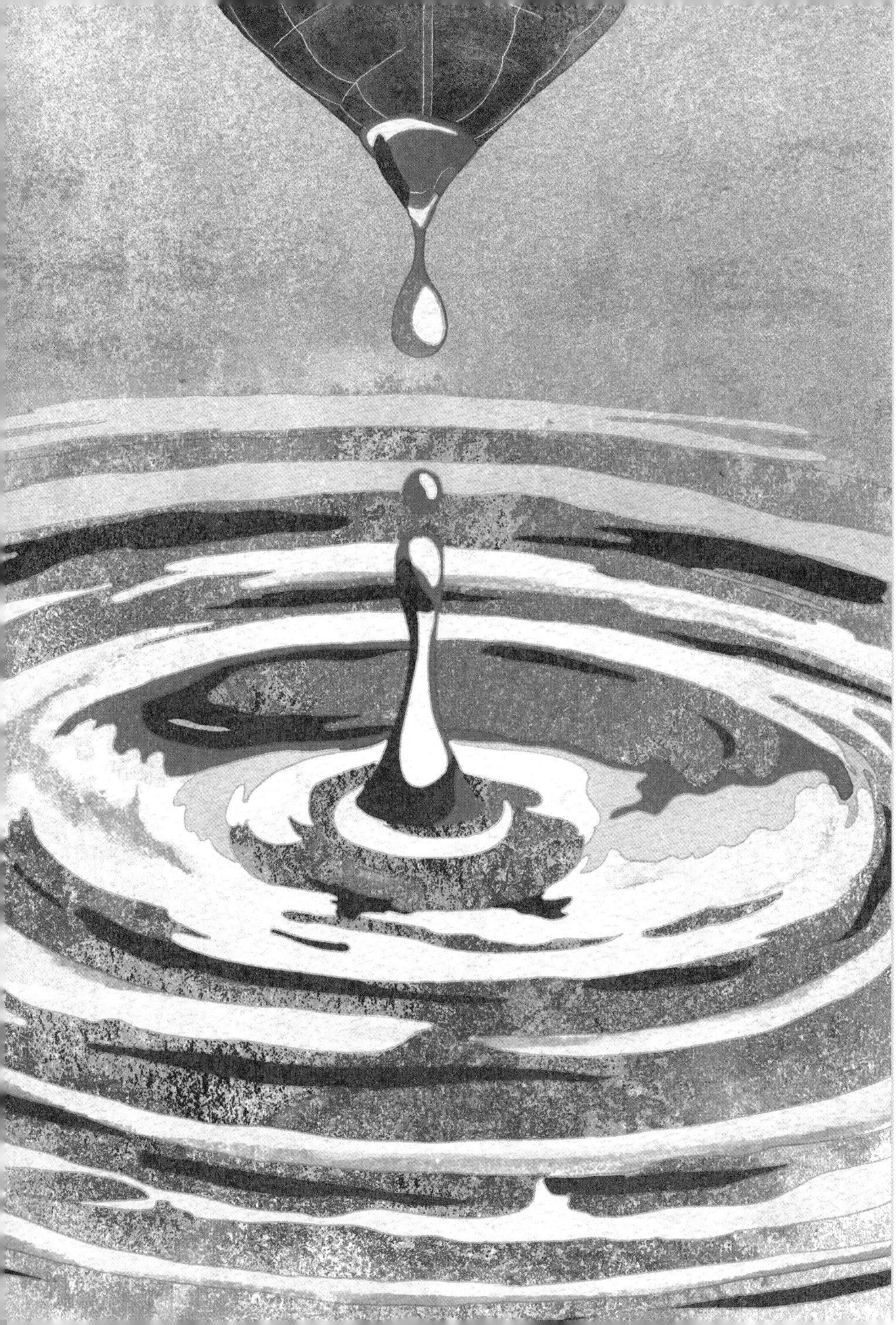

LOVE YOUR SKIN

As the outer layer and largest organ of the body, our skin often reveals how we are feeling deep inside. By creating a mindful relationship with our skin, we can accept how we look and feel in the present moment. Use this Reiki-infused ritual to share kindness with your face and body.

NEED TO KNOW

BENEFITS Helps you connect to your skin in the present moment; sends love and compassion to your skin.

TIME Be guided by Reiki.

PREPARATION In a quiet place, close your eyes, put your hands in *gasshō* (see pages 30–31) and connect to Reiki. Take deep, slow breaths into your *hara*.

01

Visualize yourself as the sun rises, sitting near a clear stream. Imagine rubbing wet earth into your skin, let it dry, then gently wash it away. Feel a warm glow inside and around you. Notice and accept any feelings that arise.

02

Bring your hands to your face and share Reiki, still visualizing this freeing, warm space. When you are ready, bring your hands down to your heart-space. Take a slow breath and feel deep gratitude for your skin in the present moment.

03

When you are ready, open your eyes and say three times, "I am beautiful and I am enough". Put your hands in *gasshō*. Thank Reiki.

TAKE A REIKI BATH

A Reiki bath is a wonderful way to relax and recharge your energy levels. This practice uses the same hand positions as the full treatment on pages 42–57. To enhance the experience, you could choose to play soothing music, fill the space with candles and crystals, or add essential oils or flower petals to the water.

01

Allow your breath to flow naturally. As you breathe, feel your body wind down and your mind become calm and clear of distractions.

NEED TO KNOW

BENEFITS Deep relaxation and cleansing; purification; recharged energy levels.

TIME 30 minutes; longer if needed.

PREPARATION Fill a bath with warm water and prepare your space as you wish. Lie in the bath, close your eyes, put your hands in *gasshō* and connect with Reiki (see pages 30–31).

02

Starting at your crown, follow the hand positions of the full treatment, spending around 3 minutes on each of your chakras.

03

Place your left hand on your heart and your right hand on or over your *hara*. Breathe Reiki in through your hands (see pages 32–33) and imagine your body filling with healing, white light.

04

Be still and follow your breath as you bathe in the healing glow. Allow the light to circulate throughout your entire body and infuse every part of your being. When you are ready, recite the five Reiki principles (see pages 26–27).

05

Take three deep breaths into your *hara*, then exhale with an "Ahhh" sound. When you are ready, let the water drain as you place your hands in *gasshō* and thank Reiki.

FOREST BATHING

Shinrin-yoku ("forest bathing") is a traditional healing technique in Japanese folk medicine. By lying down in woodland, we receive healing from the surrounding trees. As we practise this exercise and connect to Reiki, we bridge any separation that exists in our lives and reconnect with nature.

01

Find a place outdoors, ideally in a wood or forest, where you can lie down safely. Connect to *gasshō* (see pages 30–31) to centre yourself and bring your awareness to your breath.

NEED TO KNOW

BENEFITS Inner peace; a sense of rejuvenation and deep gratitude.

TIME Start with 10 minutes; build up to 30 minutes or more.

02

Take a deep breath and allow the energy of Reiki to guide you as you connect to the spirit of the trees. Let their trunks remind you that you are strong; let their roots help you feel grounded.

03

Keep breathing deeply, connecting to the Earth's energy and allowing nature to heal and support you. Place your hands on your *hara* and say the affirmation, "I am connected to the spirit of the trees". Notice any sensations that arise as you surrender and lie in stillness.

04

When you are ready, let go of the affirmation. Continue to breathe in the nature that surrounds you for as long as you feel you need to.

05

To finish the session, place your hands in *gasshō* and thank Reiki.

NEW MOON INTENTION

The New Moon is a time of beginnings and renewed energy – and for setting intentions for the things we wish to call into our lives. Practise this ritual monthly and tune into your inner wisdom, true passions, and purposes.

NEED TO KNOW

BENEFITS Helps us take responsibility for our lives and be accountable for our actions; each cycle of the Moon allows us the opportunity to grow and transform.

TIME As long as needed. Perform monthly, on the evening of the New Moon.

ITEMS NEEDED Notepad; pen; white candle.

PREPARATION Light the candle and place it in front of you. Put your hands in *gasshō* (see pages 30–31) and connect to Reiki. Take three deep breaths into your *hara*.

01

Close your eyes and ask out loud, "What would I like to call into my life under this New Moon?" Remain in the flow of Reiki for at least 15 minutes to let your thoughts arise.

02

Open your eyes and write down your intentions. With a hand on or over the list, send Reiki. Read the list aloud and send your intentions into the universe. Take a deep breath into your *hara*, and say, "And so it is".

03

You can keep the list in a safe space or safely burn it. Place one hand on your heart and the other on your *hara*. Take a breath and feel the connection to the candlelight and to your new intentions. When you feel ready, blow out the candle.

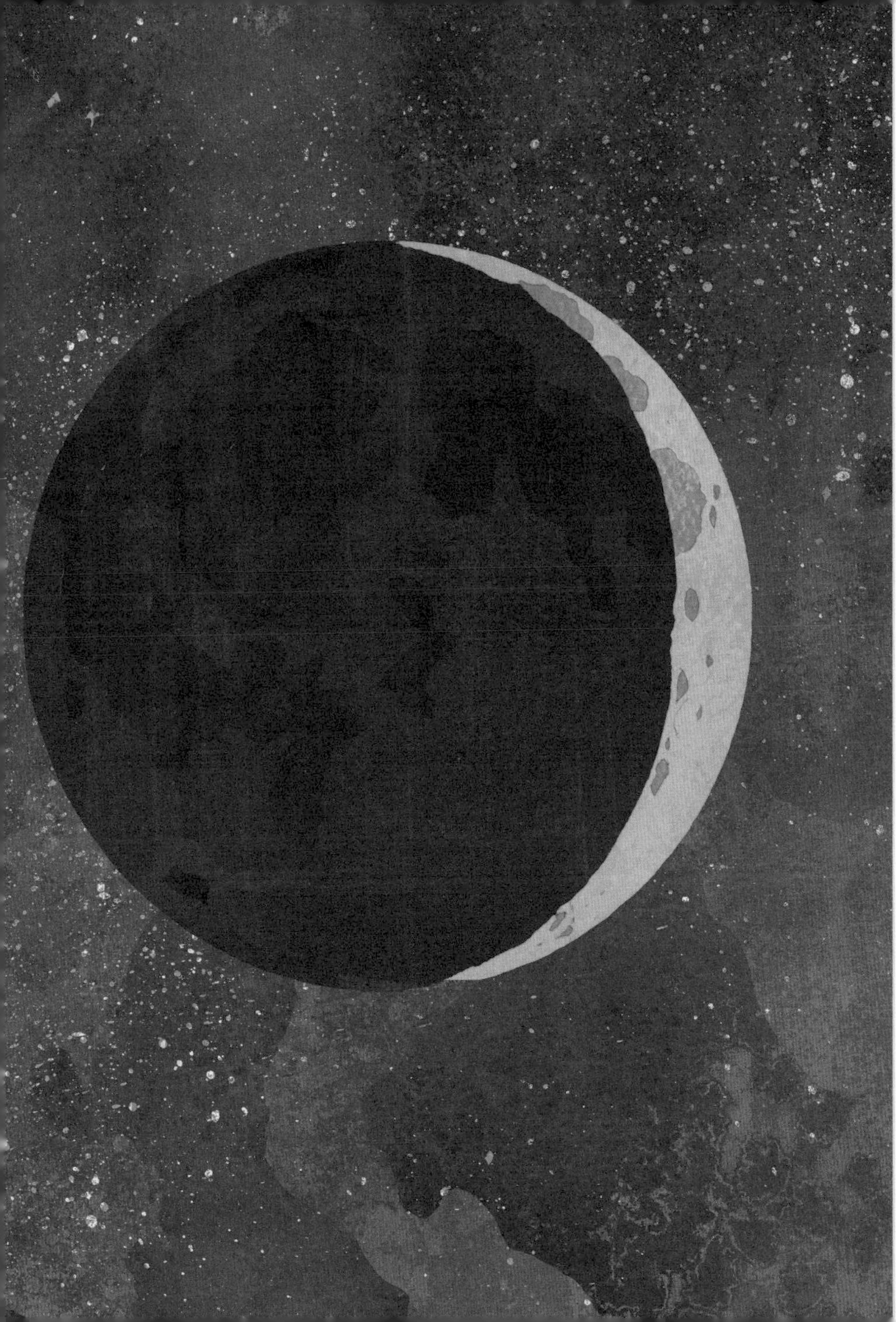

FULL MOON INTENTION

We are cyclic beings, and can grow and develop by following the Moon's cycles. The Full Moon is a time to release thoughts and intentions that no longer serve us. By setting intentions for things that we would like to let go of, we make room for fresh energy and renewed ambitions.

02

Take a deep breath into your *hara* and open your eyes. Write your intentions down, then place both hands on or over the paper and send Reiki.

01

Close your eyes and ask yourself, "What would I like to let go of under this Full Moon?" Stay connected to Reiki and allow time for your feelings to form.

NEED TO KNOW

BENEFITS Support in celebrating letting go of what no longer serves you; healing; motivation and self-improvement.

TIME 20 minutes (longer if needed); perform the ritual monthly, under a Full Moon.

ITEMS NEEDED Notepad; pen; frankincense oil or resin and burner.

PREPARATION Burn a little frankincense and place it in front of you. Put your hands in *gasshō* (see pages 30–31) and connect to Reiki. Take three deep breaths into your *hara*.

03

With intention, read the list aloud then say, "And so it is". With your hands in *gasshō*, send gratitude to the Moon and Reiki. Safely burn the list.

04

Place one hand on your heart and the other on your *hara*. Take a deep, healing breath and feel the connection with the Full Moon.

GROUNDING

When you are feeling unbalanced, grounding helps you to feel rooted in your body. This exercise is useful after deep meditation – helping you to come "back to earth" when tuning in to your intuition or psychic abilities. Take time to allow your deep connection with Mother Earth to develop fully.

NEED TO KNOW

BENEFITS Stabilizes energy to help you feel calm and centred in your body. Helps to relieve anxiety and depression.

TIME 10 minutes a day (longer if needed).

PREPARATION Sit, stand or lie comfortably. Close your eyes and connect to *gasshō* (see pages 30–31). Place both hands on your *hara* (see picture opposite).

FURTHER PRACTICE Reiki 2+ practitioners can use the power symbol (see pages 38–39).

01

Take a deep breath into your *hara* and say, "Breathing in". On the out-breath, exhale any stagnant energy and say, "Breathing out".

02

Visualize yourself firmly rooted into the ground, with a cord that runs from your *hara* deep into the earth below. Sense the grounding of your body, mind, and soul.

03

Feel grounded and connected in the moment, just as you are. Take a deep breath into your *hara*, then fully breathe out. Place your hands in *gasshō* and open your eyes.

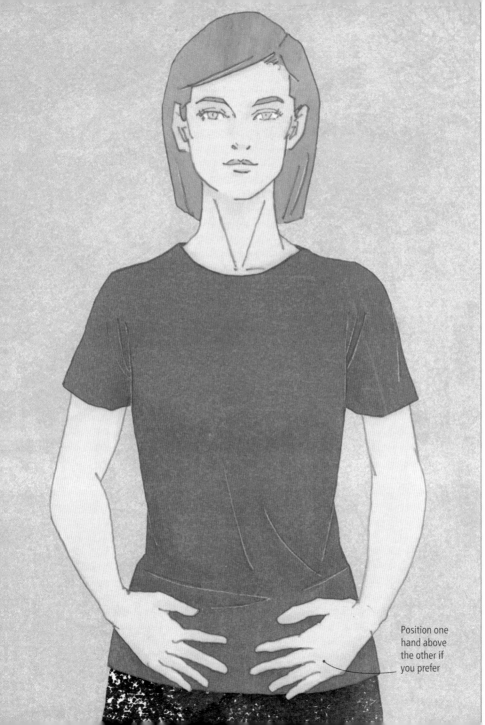

Position one
hand above
the other if
you prefer

02

Visualize yourself as you are now,
or as your younger self. Repeat
the phrases over and over,
allowing your loving kindness
to permeate your entire being.
As you recite, feel your heart
open and receive Reiki.

01

Place both hands on or over
your heart and feel it soften.
Recite these words to yourself:
"May I be filled with love and
kindness. May I be happy. May I
be well and healthy. May I be
safe and at peace".

AWAKENING YOUR HEART

Metta is a meditation that connects us with our heart *ki*,
using words, images, and feelings to send loving kindness
to ourselves and others. Regularly connecting in this way
can be a transformational experience – use a journal to
record your heart experiences and the guidance offered to
you, to help you apply it in your life.

03

Extend the meditation to your loved ones, then to all living beings, and finally to the universe. Do this by reciting the words in step 1, replacing "I" first with "you", and then with "they".

04

Be patient as you journey through this healing meditation. Take time to overcome any resistance, and to notice any guidance that is offered to you.

05

To finish the meditation, put your hands in *gasshō* and thank Reiki, with a deep sense of gratitude.

NEED TO KNOW

BENEFITS Helps you listen and live from the heart, where our true self, passions and purpose lie; fosters peace, compassion, and kindness.

TIME 25 minutes or longer if needed.

PREPARATION Find a comfortable, safe space. Sit on a chair or lie on the floor, and close your eyes, and breathe. Allow your body to relax. Position your hands in *gasshō* (see pages 30–31) and spend a few minutes connecting to Reiki.

CONNECT TO YOUR INTUITION

Our Third Eye connects us to Heaven energy and the spirit realm. The meditation *Reiji Hō* ("guided by spirits") helps you open up to your higher consciousness and intuition.

NEED TO KNOW

BENEFITS Regular practice strengthens your intuition; deepens spiritual connection.

TIME Take as long as you need – this meditation can take practice.

PREPARATION Sit or lie down comfortably. Close your eyes, put your hands in *gasshō* (see pages 30–31) and connect to Reiki.

01

Keeping your hands in *gasshō*, move them slowly up to your Third Eye. Now bring your hands over your Third Eye and breathe Reiki into it, through your hands. Ask the spirits to guide you to anywhere that needs healing, or answer questions on which you need guidance.

02

Move your hands to where you have been guided, and share Reiki. If you sense there are more areas to heal, continue sharing Reiki until you are finished.

03

To complete the meditation, put your hands in *gasshō* and thank Reiki.

Hands are placed
over the Third Eye
(see pages 46–47)

MORNING MEDITATION

This beautiful meditation is called *Hatsurei Hō* ("purifying the spirit"). It is a good technique for a morning ritual because it reconnects you to your own being, intuition, heart and soul, and fosters your connection to nature and living things, giving you focus for the day ahead.

01

Place a few drops of essential oil into your palms and massage your hands together. Cup your hands over your nose and inhale gently a few times.

NEED TO KNOW

BENEFITS Aligns and removes blockages of the mind, body, and spirit; cleanses and invigorates; deepens spiritual practice.

TIME 15 minutes; longer if required.

ITEMS NEEDED Sweet orange essential oil (organically sourced).

CAUTION Do not use essential oils if you are pregnant, unless under the guidance of a qualified aromatherapist.

02

Begin by performing dry
bathing (see pages 60–61).
Sit or lie comfortably with
your hands in your lap,
palms up. Spend a few
minutes breathing Reiki
into your *hara*.

03

Place your hands in *gasshō*,
in front of your heart. Visualize
breathing Reiki deeper and
deeper through your hands
into your heart-space.
Continue for 5–10 minutes.

04

As you exhale, visualize
sending Reiki energy out from
your heart to your entire being.
After a few minutes, send Reiki
out into your aura.

05

After a few more minutes,
extend Reiki out into the
space around you and
beyond, into the world and
then to the whole universe.
Finish in *gasshō* and
thank Reiki.

02
——

Sit comfortably, put your hands in *gasshō* (see pages 30–31) and sense Reiki. Now place your hands on your lap, with your palms facing down.

01
——

Pour a few drops of oil into your palms and massage your hands together. Cup your hands over your nose and inhale gently a few times.

AFTERNOON MEDITATION

By the afternoon, we often feel our energy and spirits begin to flag. This meditation, *Koki Hō* ("healing with the breath"), allows us to share Reiki with the breath, making it easy to practise, even in public places.

03
Notice where in your mind or body you feel the need to send Reiki. Breathe in through your nose, filling your *hara*, diaphragm, and lungs with Reiki.

04
Make an "O" shape with your mouth. Then exhale slowly and fully, sending Reiki with your breath to any area that needs attention.

05
When you feel ready to finish, put your hands in *gasshō* and thank Reiki.

NEED TO KNOW

BENEFITS Helps you reset yourself and feel centred; improves energy levels, concentration, and motivation.

TIME As much time as you need.

ITEMS NEEDED Peppermint essential oil (organically sourced).

CAUTION If you feel light-headed, stop and allow your breathing to return to normal. Only start again when you feel completely better. Do not use essential oils if you are pregnant, unless under the guidance of a qualified aromatherapist.

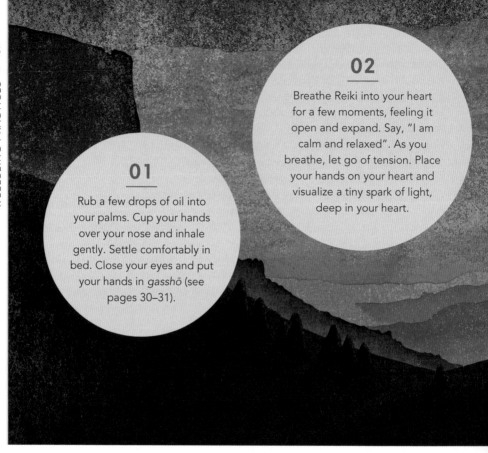

02

Breathe Reiki into your heart for a few moments, feeling it open and expand. Say, "I am calm and relaxed". As you breathe, let go of tension. Place your hands on your heart and visualize a tiny spark of light, deep in your heart.

01

Rub a few drops of oil into your palms. Cup your hands over your nose and inhale gently. Settle comfortably in bed. Close your eyes and put your hands in *gasshō* (see pages 30–31).

EVENING MEDITATION

Sleep is essential for health and wellbeing, but many of us struggle to switch off from everyday worries and reconnect with ourselves. Practise this meditation regularly, taking your time over each step, to wind down fully and prepare yourself for restful, refreshing sleep.

03

Now recite, "I am light".
Visualize the spark growing
brighter within your heart, then
radiating outwards to warm your
whole body. Expand the light into
your aura, the surrounding space,
and then to all living things.

04

Bring your awareness back to
your heart and see the spark of
light there. Know that you can
return to this state of peace and
connection whenever you need
to. Put your hands in *gasshō*
and thank Reiki. Sleep well.

NEED TO KNOW

BENEFITS Helps to quiet the mind and relax the body; deepens
spiritual practice, encouraging good quality sleep and vivid
dreams; establishes a healthy sleep routine.

TIME 15 minutes; longer if needed.

ITEMS NEEDED Frankincense essential oil (organically sourced).

CAUTION Do not use essential oils if you are pregnant, unless
under the guidance of a qualified aromatherapist.

UNBLOCK YOUR ENERGY

This healing meditation uses breath to share Reiki with our seven chakras to release any stagnant energy, leaving us feeling renewed and balanced. Take time to allow Reiki energy to bathe each chakra in turn, feeling them soften and expand in the healing light.

03

Move on to your solar plexus chakra, seat of personal power. Breathe healing light into the space and repeat: "I am worthy of pursuing my passions and purpose".

02

When you are ready, bring awareness to your sacral chakra, the centre of emotional intelligence. Visualize light expanding into the area and repeat: "I am the creator of my entire reality".

01

Breathe Reiki into your root chakra, where the weight of your body rests. Repeat: "I am grounded, supported, and abundant".

NEED TO KNOW

BENEFITS Clears blockages; allows energy to flow, cleansing and supporting you physically, mentally, emotionally, and spiritually. Connects you to your intuition.

TIME As long as needed; be guided by Reiki.

PREPARATION If you need to, remind yourself of your 7 chakras (see pages 42–43). In a quiet place, sit with a straight spine and close your eyes. Put your hands in *gasshō* (see pages 30–31) and connect to Reiki.

04

Shift attention to your
heart chakra. Breathe Reiki
into it and repeat: "I am love,
I give love, I am open to love".
Now move up to your throat, the
chakra of personal will. Repeat:
"I express myself freely".

05

Bring awareness to your Third Eye,
home of your intuition. Breathe
into it and repeat: "I trust my
intuition". Finally, breathe into your
crown chakra, your centre of
oneness, and repeat:
"The universe supports me".

06

Sense that your chakras
are now aligned and
balanced. Recite the
affirmation: "I am
whole". Finish with your
hands in *gasshō*.

CLEAR YOUR SPACE

Reiki can clear spaces of stagnant, old, and low vibrations and energies. These can be left behind by people, technology, the environment, or past events. This exercise uses *Byōsen*, a technique of using intuition to scan for negative energy fields. Make this part of your cleaning routine, or use it before moving in to a new space.

02

Intuitively and slowly, scan the space. If you sense any stagnant energy, visualize collecting it and bringing it to the centre of the space.

01

Take 3 deep, slow breaths into your *hara*. Feel yourself grounded and supported by the universe. Now visualize yourself creating a portal down to the Earth's core.

NEED TO KNOW

BENEFITS Brings renewed energy, makes your space feel lighter; supports you in clearing own own energy blockages.

TIME Be guided by Reiki; time taken will depend on the size of the space.

PREPARATION Perform the dry-bathing exercise (see pages 60–61). Stand in the centre of the space, put your hands in *gasshō* (see pages 30–31), and connect to Reiki.

03

Continue until you have gathered all the negative energy in the space. Now send all of it through the portal, deep into the Earth. Imagine Reiki recycling and renewing the old energies into high vibrations and light energy.

04

Sense the space around you feeling lighter and brighter. To finish, take 3 deep, slow breaths into your *hara*, and perform the dry-bathing ritual again. Connect to *gasshō* and thank Reiki.

EXPAND YOUR SPIRITUALITY

Practise this meditation regularly to deepen your connection with the Earth, Heaven, and Heart *ki* through your three *tanden* points – the three energy centres that reside in your physical body.

NEED TO KNOW

BENEFITS Develops spiritual growth; deepens meditation practice; boosts physical, emotional and spiritual wellbeing.

TIME 35 minutes.

PREPARATION In a quiet space, sit with a straight spine, with your feet on the ground and eyes closed. Put your hands in *gasshō* (see pages 30–31), connect to Reiki, and breathe slowly in and out through your nose.

01

Place your hands on or over your *hara*. Visualize breathing white light into it, more deeply with each breath, for 10 minutes. Notice any feelings or sensations that arise.

02

Put your hands on or over your heart, the centre of your emotions. Repeat the breathing and visualization process in step 1.

03

Place your hands on or over your Third Eye, and connect to your intuition. Repeat the breathing and visualization process.

04

Connect by spending 5 minutes breathing through all 3 energy centres. Finish by putting your hands in *gasshō* and thanking Reiki.

02

On your next breath, exhale audibly with a releasing "Aahhh" sound Sense that your aura is now illuminated by white light.

01

Rest your hands on your lap, palms upwards. Breathe in slowly and deeply, visualizing brilliant white light flowing into your *hara* as you inhale. Now breathe out, letting go of any tension you feel.

CONNECT TO YOUR SPIRIT GUIDES

Spirit guides, whether they are angels, magical beings, or loved ones who have passed, can be called on to guide and empower you on life's journey. Use this meditation to connect to these spirits – as your intuition develops, you may find your own ways to communicate with them.

03

With eyes closed, look up through your Third Eye and feel it open and expand as brilliant light pours in. Make contact with your spirit guides by saying: "Dear guides of the highest truth and compassion, I welcome you to connect with me now".

04

Still breathing deeply, spend time with your guides. If you don't sense them immediately, have the intention and trust that they are with you. When you are ready, finish by placing your hands in *gasshō*. Thank Reiki and your guides.

NEED TO KNOW

BENEFITS Enhances spiritual awakening and the self-healing experience.

TIME Be guided by Reiki.

PREPARATION Find a quiet, undisturbed place. Sit with your eyes closed, and breathe slowly through your nose. Put your hands in *gasshō* (see pages 30–31) and connect to Reiki.

CAUTION At first this exercise may feel overwhelming, but give yourself time. Be patient and regularly practise connecting with your guides.

HEALING
PRACTICES

02

Place both your hands over the area where you are feeling the most pain, discomfort or tension. Visualize Reiki energy bathing the area with healing light.

01

Breathe slowly and deeply. Each time you exhale, feel yourself more relaxed. Set an intention that you would like to ease the pain you are experiencing.

MANAGE YOUR PAIN

Practising Reiki can activate natural self-healing. Daily meditation can also help your body to cope with physical discomfort. Pain in one area is often a sign of something wrong elsewhere that we are suppressing – use this gentle meditation to check in with your body and listen to what it is telling you.

03

Stay in this position for as long as you need to. Listen to your body and notice any changes to your pain level. If there is no immediate improvement, trust that with regular treatments, the pain will eventually ease.

04

When you are ready to end the meditation, place your hands in *gasshō* and thank Reiki.

NEED TO KNOW

BENEFITS Eases physical pain and tension, promoting better sleep, greater energy and improved mood.

TIME 15–60 minutes.

PREPARATION Find a comfortable, quiet place. Put your hands in *gasshō* (see pages 30–31), take deep, slow breaths into your *hara*, and connect to Reiki.

CAUTION If your pain continues or increases, speak to your doctor.

RELIEVE YOUR BACK PAIN

Back trouble is often not just a physical issue. We hold emotional stress in our backs – financial worries, poor work-life balance, or emotional baggage can lead to pain and stiffness. This meditation supports you in caring for your back.

NEED TO KNOW

BENEFITS Relieves pain by clearing blockages and opening your intuition to connect to the pain's source.

TIME 25 minutes; longer if needed. Practise daily for maximum benefit.

PREPARATION Sit up comfortably or lie down if this is too painful. Close your eyes, place your hands in *gasshō* (see pages 30–31), breathe into your *hara*, and connect to Reiki.

CAUTION If your pain continues or increases, talk to your doctor.

01

Set an intention to ease the pain you are feeling. Breathe slowly and deeply, visualizing Reiki energy flowing into your *hara*. Feel your breath expanding to bring healing light into your back. Continue for 5–10 minutes.

02

Still breathing Reiki into the area, bring your hands round to your lower back. Stay like this for 20 minutes or longer. If your hands get tired, rest them for a few minutes, staying focused on sending Reiki.

03

When you are ready to finish, take 3 breaths into your *hara*, place your hands in *gasshō* and thank Reiki.

Rest your thumbs on your sides and spread your fingers

SUPPORT YOUR DIGESTION

This meditation focuses on the health of your gut, stimulating a sluggish system and soothing irritation or inflammation. It is especially helpful for settling nausea or an upset stomach.

NEED TO KNOW

BENEFITS Sending Reiki energy boosts the digestive system and can help with other, less obvious symptoms such as fatigue and anxiety.

TIME 10 minutes, building up to 1 hour.

PREPARATION Find a quiet space and sit comfortably. Breathe slowly and deeply, put your hands in *gasshō* and connect to Reiki.

CAUTION If pain or irritation continues or increases, talk to your doctor.

01

Place both hands over or on your solar plexus chakra (see pages 52–53). Visualize breathing Reiki energy into it, from the roots of the Earth and from the sky above.

02

As the healing energy flows into your solar plexus, see it as radiant yellow – the colour of the Sun.

03

Keep breathing deeply and slowly, bathing your solar plexus with healing, yellow energy, which expands with every breath.

04

Continue for as long as you need. To finish, place your hands in *gasshō* and thank Reiki.

Fingers are touching or interlinked

02

Intend to extend Reiki into
every layer – emotional,
physical, mental, and spiritual
– then into your aura, your
bedroom, and the space
beyond. You are breathing
light and love.

01

In bed, rest your arms by your
sides with palms up, and take
a few minutes to do a full
body scan. Starting from the
soles of your feet, share Reiki
with every part of your body,
to the top of your head.

ENJOY BETTER SLEEP

Use this Reiki meditation in your sleep journey, to find
tranquility and calm through universal energy, visualization,
and silence. Try it after taking a Reiki bath (see pages
80–81), and use your out-breaths to let go of anything that
no longer serves you.

03

If you wish, place a hand on or over your heart and *hara*. Breathing in a gentle rhythm, visualize the vast, dark sky above you, and the bright stars in the sky beaming down their healing light.

04

Continuing to be aware of your breath, recite the affirmation: "I am peace, calm, and love". Repeat for as long you feel you need to.

05

When you have finished, bathe in the light of the stars. Lie in stillness and silence until sleep comes naturally.

NEED TO KNOW

BENEFITS Clears the mind, reduces stress and worry.

TIME Be guided by Reiki.

PREPARATION In a quiet, darkened bedroom, lie down in bed, relax, and close your eyes. Place your hands in *gasshō* (see pages 30–31) and connect to Reiki.

SOOTHE A HEADACHE

This treatment helps to relieve the stress and tension that cause headaches and migraines. We breathe in Reiki to oxygenate the mind and body, then breathe out toxins and what no longer serves us. Before you begin, you may also choose to set an intention to improve clarity, concentration, and flow.

02

Spend 10 minutes breathing Reiki. Then put your right hand on top of your head and your left hand on the back of your head.

NEED TO KNOW

BENEFITS Eases tension headaches and migraines.

TIME Up to an hour, or until the pain eases.

PREPARATION Sit or lie down comfortably in a quiet, darkened space. Place your hands in *gasshō* and connect to Reiki.

CAUTION If your pain continues or increases, talk to your doctor.

01

Take a few deep breaths into your *hara*, then extend the breath up into your solar plexus, then further up to your Third Eye (see page 43 for chakra locations).

03
___

Continue in this position, breathing healing energy into your headspace, for up to 45 minutes. For a migraine, spend 15 minutes like this, then put your hands over your temples for 15 minutes, and over your eyes for 15 minutes more.

04
___

Finish by putting your hands in *gasshō* and thanking Reiki. If you can, allow space and time for healing rest or sleep.

RELIEVE COLDS AND FLU

We can support our immune system by regularly performing a full Reiki treatment (see pages 42–57), but in a busy world, colds and viruses are hard to avoid. This exercise can help to relieve the symptoms of colds or flu, and is excellent for viral infections, sinusitis, and hayfever too.

NEED TO KNOW

BENEFITS Helps to alleviate symptoms such as high temperature, sore throat, blocked nose, and chesty cough.

TIME 25 minutes, plus time for rest afterwards. Take around 5 minutes for each step.

ITEMS NEEDED A few drops of organic Japanese mint oil or eucalyptus essential oil, in a diffuser.

PREPARATION Lie down in a quiet place and switch on the diffuser. Close your eyes, place your hands in *gasshō* (see pages 30–31), and connect to Reiki. Set an intention to allow yourself time and space to feel better, supported by Reiki.

CAUTION Do not use essential oils if you are pregnant, unless under the guidance of a qualified aromatherapist.

02

Place a hand on or over each ear and send healing energy to this area. Breathe and enjoy the oil's soothing vapours.

01

Place both hands on or over your crown (see page 43) and share Reiki. After 5 minutes, put a hand on or over each eye, and stay like this, sharing Reiki.

03

Now place your right hand on or over the back of your neck, and your left hand on or over your throat.

04

Move your left hand to your heart and your right hand to your chest. Continue to feel Reiki flow through your hands.

05

To finish, lie with your arms by your sides, palms upwards. Relax and, if you can, sleep. Reiki will keep flowing to heal and soothe.

02

Breathe Reiki, starting from the soles of your feet, through your solar plexus to the top of your head. Breathe in for 4 counts, hold the breath for 4 counts, and exhale for 4 counts, letting go of whatever no longer serves you.

01

If you wish, call on your spirit guides for support. Place your right hand on or over your crown, and your left hand on or over your solar plexus (see page 43).

LIFT YOUR MOOD

Reiki teaches us that the connectedness of universal energy means we are never alone, even when we feel depressed or hopeless. By tapping into low vibrations, you can remove blockages to reveal the power, wisdom, and love that reside within.

03

Continue breathing in this way, taking time to sense that the light you are breathing has expanded into your aura and the space around you.

04

Recite: "I am powerful". Repeat this affirmation for 10 minutes. When you have had more practice, you can extend the time to 20 minutes.

05

Place your hands in *gasshō* and think of 3 things you are grateful for today. Thank Reiki and finish with more dry bathing.

NEED TO KNOW

BENEFITS Reduces symptoms of depression; releases feel-good hormones; raises vibrations.

TIME 15–25 minutes (be guided by Reiki).

PREPARATION In a quiet place, perform dry bathing (see pages 60–61). Sit or lie down and close your eyes. Put your hands in *gasshō* (see pages 30–31) and connect with Reiki.

CAUTION You may initially feel worse as feelings and emotions are released. If this does not pass, seek professional care.

RELEASE ANXIETY

Anxiety, stemming from emotional, mental, physical, and spiritual issues, affects us all at some point. It can have a harmful impact on mental health, sleep, concentration, digestion and more. By focusing on our breath, adopting a positive mindset, and sharing Reiki, we are better able to cope with worries and stress.

NEED TO KNOW

BENEFITS Soothes panic and distress; reduces the effects of anxiety, leading to higher concentration levels, better sleep, and improved wellbeing.

TIME Be guided by Reiki.

PREPARATION Turn to the five Reiki principles in this book, on pages 26–27. Lie comfortably, with your arms by your sides, palms up, and connect to Reiki.

03

Come back to your natural breathing and rest in this space for 5 minutes, allowing peace to fill your mind, body, and spirit.

02

Continue this breath flow for 5 minutes. At the same time, put your palms behind your head and visualize the healing light flowing out of your palms and into your headspace.

01

Inhale through your nose for a count of 5, hold for 3, then exhale for 5 through your mouth with a "Ssss" sound, relaxing the jaw, shoulders, and stomach. Visualize white, healing light filling your *hara*, chest, and lungs.

04

Put your hands on your heart. Breathe in healing energy and breathe out the thoughts and feelings that no longer serve you. Feel the support of Reiki as it fills your heart and expands, out of your body into the space around you.

05

For about 5 minutes recite the Reiki principles, guided by your breath and Reiki. Finish by placing hands in *gasshō* (see pges 30–31) and thanking Reiki.

02

Now place one hand on or over the part of your body that needs attention. Share Reiki for 15–20 minutes, with the intention for Reiki to heal the injury.

01

Breathe deeply and slowly into your *hara*, to ground you. Then breathe in for a count of 4, then out for 4. Share Reiki for 15–20 minutes, continuing the breathing pattern and staying in the moment.

REIKI FIRST-AID HEALING

Think of this meditation as part of your Reiki first-aid kit for minor accidents such as cuts and bruises, and to speed up healing or support more serious conditions. It is also effective for post-operative recovery, and during long-term treatments.

03

If your mind wanders, bring your attention back to your breath. Check for improvement, either by looking at the site or by using your intuition to sense any changes.

04

If you feel the need, continue sharing Reiki until you are ready to stop. To finish, put your hands in *gasshō* and thank Reiki.

NEED TO KNOW

BENEFITS Supports and speeds up the body's natural ability to heal. Grounding, soothing, and calming.

TIME Be guided by Reiki; perform the process as often as required.

PREPARATION Put your hands in *gasshō* (see pages 30–31), and connect to Reiki.

CAUTION If you are bleeding or experiencing dizziness, breathlessness, or chest pain, seek immediate medical advice. If pain continues or increases, talk to your doctor.

MEDITATION FOR RENEWAL

As we age, our body systems start to slow down. Reiki supports you by re-energizing cells and boosting renewal and healing processes. By entering a state of *kokoro* (pure consciousness) we can sense where to send healing energy.

NEED TO KNOW

BENEFITS Strengthens intuition; Supports body, mind, and spirit through the aging process; revives energy.

TIME 30 minutes.

PREPARATION Sit upright in a quiet place, put your hands in *gasshō* (see pages 30–31) and connect to Reiki. Place your hands in your lap, with your palms facing up.

01

Take deep, slow breaths in and out through the nose. Breath into your *hara* in for 5 counts, hold for 3, and then out for 5. Bring awareness to the top of your head and start scanning your body, slowly, layer by layer, cell by cell, down to your feet.

02

When you feel an intuitive pull to share Reiki, stop scanning and place your hands on this area. Stay there until you know it's time to move on.

03

Keeping the breath steady, continue scanning and sharing Reiki where you sense a need. To finish, put your hands in *gasshō* and thank Reiki.

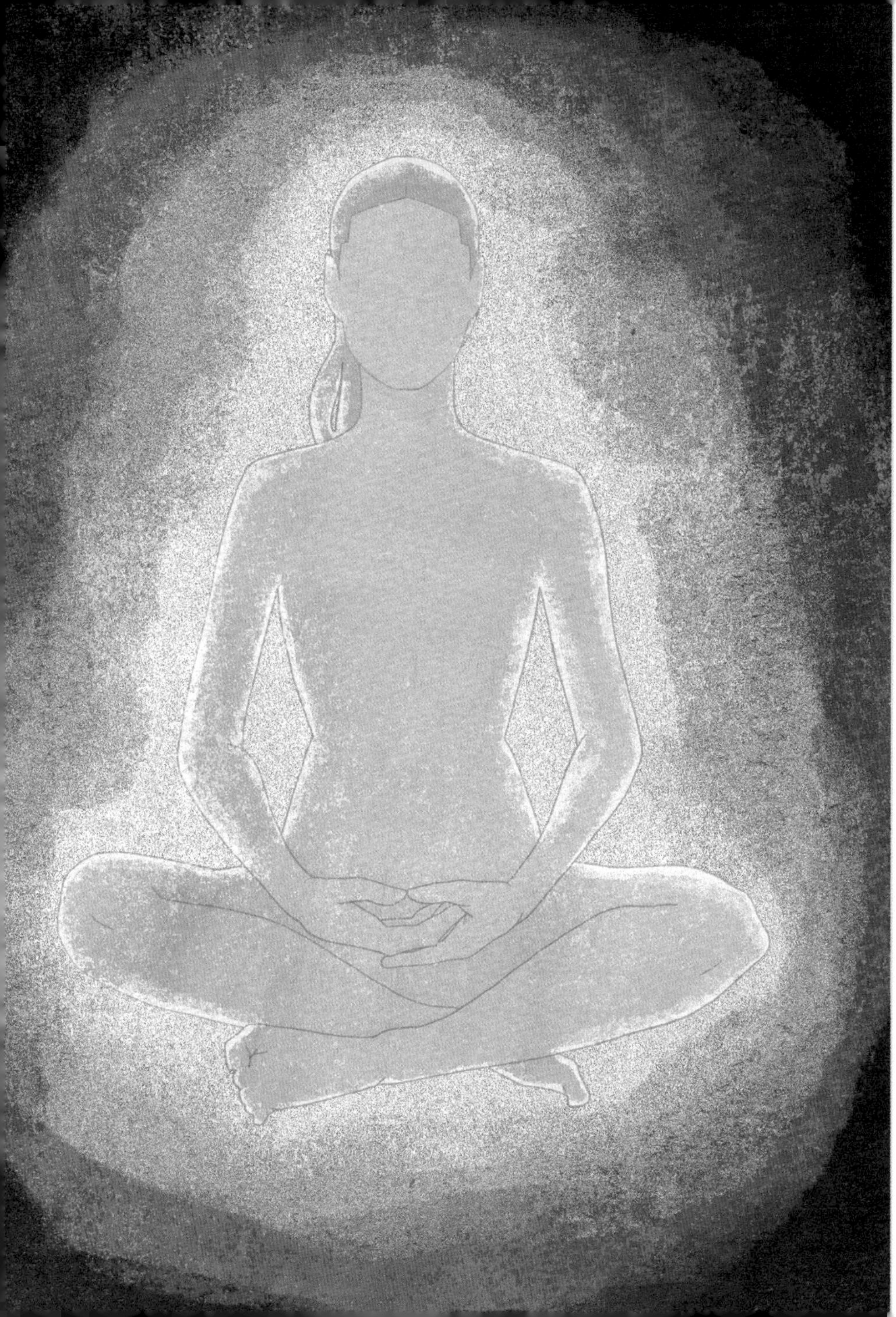

02

Breathe deeply into your heart-space and feel Reiki energy expand there. Visualize a healing, pink light flowing into your womb as an offering from your heart.

03

Stay in awareness of this pink light, opening and expanding with each breath. Tune into your senses and listen for any messages your womb may be sending you.

01

Put your right hand on or over your womb-space and your left hand on or over your heart.

WOMB-HEALING MEDITATION

This meditation supports you in journeying back into your body and reconnecting with your womb space to heal, empower, and listen to inner wisdom. Reiki energy fills your womb area with love, compassion, and kindness, whatever your stage of life.

04

After about 10 minutes, take a deep breath and exhale with an "Ahhh" sound. Place both hands on or over your womb-space, with thumbs and index fingertips touching each other to form a triangle. Share Reiki energy for another 10 minutes.

05

Draw to a close by putting your hands in *gasshō* and thanking Reiki. If you wish, make a journal of your thoughts and emotions.

NEED TO KNOW

BENEFITS Supports female and reproductive health concerns, including fertility, pregnancy, and menopause; increases confidence and purpose.

TIME Start with 20 minutes and extend to as long as you need. This meditation may be used on a New Moon to invite in new energy or on a Full Moon to let go of what no longer serves you.

PREPARATION Sitting in a quiet place, put your hands in *gasshō* (see pages 30–31) and connect with Reiki.

PARENTS' MEDITATION

Self-care is essential for new parents starting their life-changing journey. Use this meditation throughout pregnancy, then after the birth to support your own recovery and help bond with your baby. Continue with it as your baby grows, to provide comfort and positivity, helping your child thrive.

NEED TO KNOW

BENEFITS Strengthens the parent-child bond; builds parents' confidence; may help ease colic, teething, and eating problems; promotes deeper sleep and overall wellbeing.

TIME 15 minutes, if you can.

PREPARATION If you can, sit in a quiet, comfortable place with your baby next to you. Put your hands in *gasshō* (see pages 30–31) and connect to Reiki.

ADAPTATIONS If you are pregnant, place one hand on your heart, and the other on the womb-space in step 2 and visualize connecting to your child; if you are holding your baby, visualize all the steps.

03

Take time to sense deep gratitude, for yourself and for your child in the present moment.

02

Place one hand on or over your heart and the other on or over your child's. Visualize pure, unconditional love as a light-cord, joining your hearts with an unbreakable bond.

01

For a few minutes, breathe Reiki in through your nose and let its light fill you. Exhale through your mouth, releasing any thoughts and feelings that no longer serve you.

A Return To Love Marianne Williamson

Forgiveness Iyanla Vanzant

The Miracle of Mindfulness Thich Nhat Hanh

PODCAST AND RADIO

Reiki Radio

SuperSoul Conversations

Ancient Wisdom Today

Wellness Official – Dash Radio

DIRECTORY

Shibumi – International Reiki Association
https://shibumireiki.org

UK Reiki Federation
https://www.reikifed.co.uk

The Reiki Association
https://www.reikiassociation.net

The Reiki Council
http://www.reikicouncil.org.uk/

PRIVATE SESSIONS, GROUP MEDITATIONS, TRAINING, AND OTHER TOOLS

Reiki therapy is available with Jasmin Harsono in person or at a distance.

You can also experience group meditation sessions in person or to download.
Jasmin also offers Reiki training in the UK.
For more information contact:
Jasmin Harsono
https://www.emeraldandtiger.com

International Training
International House of Reiki, https://ihreiki.com

INDEX

Index entries in **bold** indicate specific wellbeing and healing practices.

ABOUT THE AUTHOR

Jasmin Harsono is a Reiki Master/Teacher, Sonic Artist, and Intuitive Wellbeing Guide. She is the founder of Emerald and Tiger, a conscious lifestyle brand promoting positive awareness through vibrant connection to body, mind, and spirit. Led to Reiki through her own experiences of ill-health, Jasmin now supports others, guiding them to tap into their true self and to understand they have everything they need in order to live well and feel whole from the inside out. Jasmin has collaborated with brands such as Selfridges, Crabtree & Evelyn, and Goop, and has featured in *Women's Health*, *Vogue*, and *Forbes* publications Jasmin's practice is based in London, where she offers one-to-one treatments, training, wellbeing guidance, creative consultancy, group and corporate workshops, and retreats.

AUTHOR'S ACKNOWLEDGMENTS

Sincere gratitude to everyone listed for your encouragement, support and guidance with this book, and with life in general. Thank you to Mikao Usui, and Reiki. Thank you to my teachers Torsten Lange, and his family. Thank you to Frans Stiene. Thank you to my family, my husband Khonnan Harsono for supporting and believing in me. I love you. Thank you to my mother Marian Houshmand, father Mozafar Houshmand (whose spirit watches over us), mother-in-law Titiek Harsono, siblings Cathy Houshmand, Roxanne Houshmand-Howell, Jonathan Houshmand, and Jared Houshmand, my brother-in-law Will Howell, and sister-in-law Giovanna Houshmand; and my beautiful nephew and nieces Ilias, Serafina, Lucia, and Sofia. I love you all dearly. Thank you to my oldest friends, Hereity Iyasu, Endaa Benoit and Kandi Lalchan. Thank you to Kayleigh Attwood, Alex Holbrook, Millana Snow, Brighitta Moser-Clark, Katsi Yuen, Alka Sethi. Thank you to the DK team Kiron Gill, Mandy Earey, Jade Wheaton, Henrietta Drane, and Andy Chapman. Special thanks to Rona Skene and Dawn Henderson for your support and guidance. Thank you Kotaro Machiyama for your beautiful illustrations that complete the book. Lastly thank you to anyone who has come for a session, a workshop, or training, and has supported my journey.

PUBLISHER'S ACKNOWLEDGMENTS

DK would like to thank the following for their assistance in the publication of this book: Mandy Earey for going above and beyond her original brief; Jade Wheaton for design assistance; John Friend for proofreading; and Marie Lorimer for compiling the index.